JEFF GNASS

He sat up the better to look at the great mountains where they went piling back, growing darker and more savage until they finished with one jagged ridge, high up against the west. Curious secret mountains; he thought of the little he knew about them.

—*John Steinbeck*

In California's mountain ranges, every ridge, every bend in the trail, every curve in every highway unfolds a new world of scenic wonders.

A waterfall (left) tumbles over its eastern Sierra precipice toward brilliant aspens near South Lake and the Owens Valley town of Bishop. Aspen grow throughout the Sierra, northern Basin, and Klamath ranges, but are especially numerous north and south of Lake Tahoe. JAMES RANDKLEV

The South Fork of the Kings River (above) rushes beneath Grand Sentinel (8,504 feet), its sheer northern face looming 3,500 feet above Zumwalt Meadows and part of the 400,000-acre Kings Canyon National Park, which was established in 1940. Only one road penetrates the park. It remains open to traffic only during summer and runs between the giant sequoias of Grants Grove and Cedar Grove. LARRY ULRICH

Long before sunrise touches most of California (opposite page), the morning sun warms ancient bristlecone pines in the White Mountains in the foreground and caps the magnificent Palisades of the Sierra Nevada in the background across the Owens Valley. JEFF GNASS

The diversity of California's mountains is rivaled only by the diversity of their stunning vegetation.

The vivid blossoms of the hedgehog cactus (far left) in the half-million-acre Joshua Tree National Monument of the Pinto Mountains enriches the desert with color. PAT O'HARA

The rugged bark of a coast redwood (left) seems to leave this lovely rhododendron and earth itself behind as it towers into the light above. DAVID MUENCH

The bristlecone pine of the White Mountains (above), some more than four thousand years old, have helped scientists unravel the history of California. Growth rings precisely reflect past climatic conditions, even volcanic activity, and are used to verify radioactive carbon-14 dating. FRED HIRSCHMANN

Yellow-throated gilla (right), also known as mustang clover, provide a final resting place for this rustic old manzanita root in the Sierra Nevada. DAVID MUENCH

California's mountains are home to an incredible array of wildlife, some non-native, some rapidly disappearing, but most thriving.

By 1986 only five California condors (left) remained in the wild, and fewer than thirty still survived in captivity. JEFF FOOTT

A dipper (top) waits beside Alder Creek in the North Coast Ranges. Also known as the water ouzel, the robin-sized bird is among the most fascinating birds in California. It bobs up and down on spray-wet rocks and dives underneath fast-flowing streams in search of aquatic insects. LARRY ULRICH

These fallow deer (above) at Wildcat Camp near Point Reyes may be descendants of those imported to California by Randolph Hearst. STEPHEN TRIMBLE

A treed mountain lion (left) in the northern Sierra Nevada survived this encounter with man, shot only with a camera. But for many decades, the "stealthy murderers," as Theodore Roosevelt once called them, had no or minimal legal protection. Barely a decade ago, numbers had been reduced from many thousand to an estimated six hundred. RON SANFORD

A male western tanager (above), the most colorful bird in California, behaves much like a flycatcher. Perching on snags and branch tips, it flicks out after insects, catching them in flight. JAN L. WASSINK

Not surprisingly, Californians spend many of their finest hours in the mountains, retreating to forget the stress of urban life.

Hikers in the Basin Ranges near Death Valley (left) are enveloped in a stunning sunset. *RON SANFORD*

A hiker (above) pauses for a cold drink in the recently designated Trinity Alps Wilderness in northern California's lush Klamath Ranges. *JOHN GUSSMAN*

Hikers pause to savor the view (left), seemingly on top of the world. DAVID STOECKLEIN.

A blazing campfire and glowing moon (above) keep a solitary backpacker company in the John Muir Wilderness near Bishop Lake. This is California's largest wilderness, extending from the Mammoth Lakes area to near Mt. Whitney along the crest of the Sierra Nevada. PAT O'HARA

A January storm gathers in the first light of sunrise along the eastern Sierra Nevada. JEFF GNASS

Soft wisps of fog scatter before the fractured vertical walls of El Capitan in Yosemite Valley, perhaps the most well-known testimonial to the grandeur of the mountains of California.
MICHAEL S. SAMPLE

California Mountain Ranges

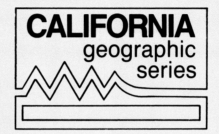

CALIFORNIA geographic series

NUMBER ONE
IN THE
CALIFORNIA GEOGRAPHIC SERIES

BY RUSSELL B. HILL

PUBLISHED BY

FALCON PRESS

About the California Geographic Series

This book, *California Mountain Ranges,* is only the beginning of the California Geographic Series, a continuing series exploring California's landscape and its inhabitants. All books in the California Geographic Series feature the finest full-color photography and a fact-filled, easy-to-read text. Upcoming books in the series will focus on California's state parks, wildlands, deserts, rivers, wildlife, coastline, and even the wondrous world which lies just offshore.

The California Geographic Series is, in essence, a portfolio of California—or better yet, a celebration. California has such incredible geographic features and diversity, and there is so much to learn. The California Geographic Series will bring that information to light in the same quality format found in this book.

These books will be collector's items. Don't miss a single one.

A dedication

To Jan,
and answers
that don't unweave the rainbow.

Acknowledgements

No mountain should be viewed from only one vantage point, and no book such as this could have been written without the perspectives added by hundreds of other mountain lovers.

The knowledge and help of Larry and Donna Ulrich (their eye for California mountains is evidenced in photographs here) was, literally, indispensable. So were the critical evaluations and suggestions of Danny Hagans, Ron Adkison, and Michael Crater, who proofread the manuscript. And, of course, so were the facts, insights, and patience so willingly contributed by innumerable public servants—chief among them the employees of our national parks and national forests, state parks, the United States Geological Survey, and the California Department of Mines and Geology.

Finally, I thank Bill Schneider and Mike Sample, and the employees of Falcon Press, for their moral as well as logistical support, and my wife, Jan, for her research, re-reading, and good humor.

California Geographic Series Staff

Publishers: Michael Sample, Bill Schneider
Editor: Bill Schneider
Photo editor: Michael Sample
Assistant photo editor: Linda Weeks
Design: Bill Schneider, Jeanette Geary, DD Dowden
Graphics: Jeanette Geary, DD Dowden, Wayne Klinkel
Marketing director: Kelly Simmons

Front Cover Photo

Banner Peak, seen from the John Muir Trail at Island Pass, looms like a stately throne above the Thousand Island Lake basin in the Ansel Adams Wilderness, Sierra Nevada. Photo by Larry Ulrich.

For more information

For general information on this book, the California Geographic Series, or other publications of Falcon Press, write Falcon Press, Marketing and Distribution, Box 279, Billings, MT 59103. Prospective authors should write to Falcon Press, Editorial and Production, P.O. Box 731, Helena, MT 59624.

Design, typesetting, graphics and other pre-press work by Falcon Press, Helena, Montana.

Library of Congress Number: 86-80188

ISBN: 0-934318-83-2 (hardcover),
0-934318-77-8 (softcover)

Printed in Japan.

Contents

Here in Rush Creek near Mono Lake—and in many similar streams—anglers find trout an irresistible mountain attraction.
MICHAEL S. SAMPLE

As dawn breaks, Lake Tahoe's celebrated Emerald Bay is temporarily misnamed. "Golden Bay" may better serve this morning.
DAVID MUENCH

The mountains of California

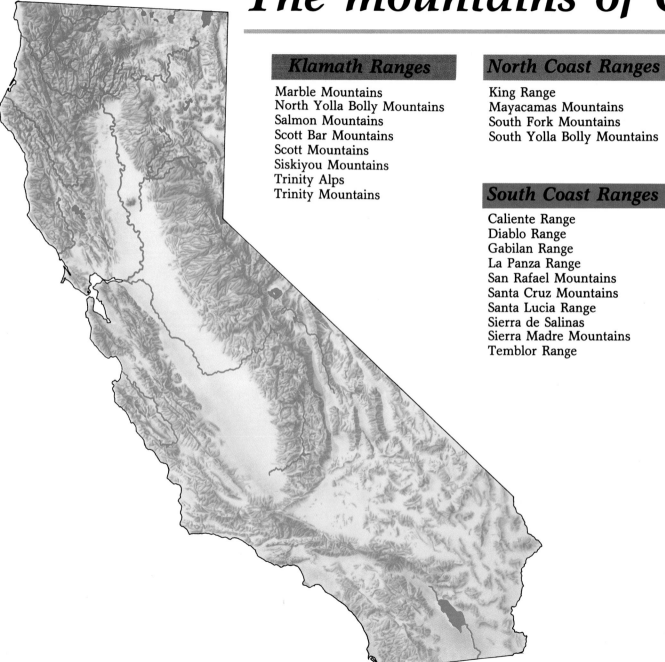

Klamath Ranges

Marble Mountains
North Yolla Bolly Mountains
Salmon Mountains
Scott Bar Mountains
Scott Mountains
Siskiyou Mountains
Trinity Alps
Trinity Mountains

North Coast Ranges

King Range
Mayacamas Mountains
South Fork Mountains
South Yolla Bolly Mountains

South Coast Ranges

Caliente Range
Diablo Range
Gabilan Range
La Panza Range
San Rafael Mountains
Santa Cruz Mountains
Santa Lucia Range
Sierra de Salinas
Sierra Madre Mountains
Temblor Range

Transverse Ranges

Little San Bernardinos
Portal Ridge Mountains
San Bernardino Mountains
San Gabriel Mountains
Santa Monica Mountains
Santa Susana Mountains
Santa Ynez Mountains
Sierra Pelona Mountains
Tehachapi Mountains
Topatopa Mountains

Peninsular Ranges

Agua Tibia Mountains
Coyote Mountains
Jacumba Mountains
Laguna Mountains
Oak Ridge Mountains
San Jacinto Mountains
San Ysidro Mountains
Santa Ana Mountains
Santa Margarita Mountains
Santa Rosa Mountains
Vallecito Mountains

Sierra Nevada

Cathedral Range
Great Western Divide
Greenhorn Mountains
Grizzly Mountains
Piute Mountains
Ritter Range
Scodie Mountains

Basin Ranges

Amargosa Range
Argus Range
Avawatz Mountains
Benton Range
Big Maria Mountains
Big Valley Mountains
Bristol Mountains
Bullion Mountains
Cady Mountains

Calico Mountains
Cargo Muchacho Mountains
Castle Mountains
Chemehuevi Mountains
Chocolate Mountains
Chuckwalla Mountains
Clark Mountain Range
Clipper Mountains
Coso Range
Cottonwood Mountains
Coxcomb Mountains
Diamond Mountains
Eagle Mountains
El Paso Mountains
Funeral Mountains
Granite Mountains (four
    separate ranges)
Grapevine Mountains
Greenwater Range
Inyo Mountains
Iron Mountains
Ivanpah Mountains
Kingston Range
Last Chance Range

Little Maria Mountains
Marble Mountains
New York Mountains
Nopah Range
Old Woman Mountains
Orocopia Mountains
Owlshead Mountains
Palen Mountains
Panamint Range
Pinto Mountains
Piute Mountains
Providence Mountains
Quail Mountains
Rand Mountains
Riverside Mountains
Sacramento Mountains
Sheep Hole Mountains
Skedaddle Mountains
Slate Range
Soda Mountains
Sweetwater Mountains
Tiefort Mountains
Turtle Mountains
Warner Range
Whipple Mountains
White Mountains

Cascade Range

Cascade Range

An introduction:

The continuing exploration

If you ask a Californian about mountains, you had better not be in a hurry. There is always, it seems, so much to tell.

If mountains were words, Californians might have the widest vocabulary on earth. Within an area of 158,693 square miles, California's mountains sport glaciers and rainforests, waterfalls and steam vents, boulder fields and grasslands. There is not a single acre within the state where mountains are not visible (except perhaps when smog intervenes), and most acres are surrounded by mountains. No other state but Alaska has more mountains; not even Alaska has such a variety of mountains.

Mountains rule California. They wring water from the clouds, decreeing lush valleys on one side and barren wastelands on the other. They are the engines powering immense transfers of water, irrigating deserts and watering lawns.

California's mountains nourish vast forests and fields, making the state a leading provider of agricultural products and lumber.

Winds do their bidding. Here, they air condition a city; there, they drown a city in smog; somewhere else, they spin turbines and create electrical power.

Yet, California's mountains are something more than benevolent dictators bestowing such favors as fertile silt and fantastic ski slopes. They determine not only our well-being, but also our *being*. A harried commuter can gaze up from traffic jams at high slopes and remember what wilderness is. A climber, sighting like a marksman through a valley at the peak beyond, can literally measure himself against the earth.

We see California's mountains, and we see from them. The photographs in these pages are vivid proof that mountains in themselves are enchanting and awful, serene and thrilling, mysterious and barren. Some are terraced as beautifully, as gently as Chinese gardens. Others merit warning signs: "This Trail is Jackassable—For Horses Impassable," or "Private Property—Stay On Road—Survivors Will Be Prosecuted."

California's mountains invite us to kneel, to inspect tiny, delicate wildflowers. And like stars and clouds, these mountains invite us to find huge images, likenesses, faces in their shapes. We cannot help but look at mountains.

We also understand mountains from above, from aerial photographs and relief maps, as we could never understand them otherwise. Seen from the mountains, the largest, most threatening metropolis seems tiny. Visitors to California's mountains leave behind a world of time clocks, computers, and calendars.

No book has ever exhausted California mountains, or ever will. *California Mountain Ranges* does not. What it does do is explore, sample, paint, and marvel at the mountains of California, perhaps glimpsing something unexpected along the way.

Unavoidably, any book such as this reflects the mountains themselves, in all their splendid beauty and inconvenient disarray. As surely as the photographs in *California Mountain Ranges* elicit awe, its text will elicit argument. Even though we

Yosemite's El Capitan (far left), 3,000 feet high and the tallest unbroken cliff on earth, is reflected in the placid Merced River. El Capitan has the oldest and strongest granite of seven types found in the Yosemite Valley.
MICHAEL S. SAMPLE

The smooth petals of mariposa lilies beneath Belle Mountain enrich the stark Pinto Mountains in Joshua Tree National Monument. The bulbs of mariposa lilies lie protected underground from heat and drought, sprouting only during moist weather to compete with perennial species.
PATTY A. FURBUSH

The morning fog (right) sets the stage for another mountain day.
CARR CLIFTON

all have different memories of "our" particular mountains, we expect to agree on the facts about those mountains—on names, for instance, or elevation figures. But California's mountains, to a great extent, have yet to be explored.

Anyone familiar with them realizes how *little* is actually known about the mountains of California. Names and elevation figures are simply the most notorious examples of irregularity. It is not uncommon to find various names and two, three, even four or more elevations cited for the same peak. Even Mt. Whitney, the state's most celebrated peak, has prompted heated arguments over its height and its name.

Finality, of course, is hardly an appropriate expectation of California mountains, for two reasons. First, these mountains are too many. They are overwhelming not only in size but also in sheer numbers, and in extent. They cover thousands of square miles and are often located in the most remote, inaccessible regions of the state.

The task of surveying these mountains is staggering, both difficult and expensive. Innumerable elevation figures still in use were recorded decades ago, with relatively crude measuring devices and methods. Experts working with the most modern equipment may be able to achieve more precision today, but they still face a vast undertaking which will not, even under ideal conditions, be completed within their lifetimes—if ever.

And the job of systemmatically cataloguing California's mountains is next to impossible, not only because of the size of the job itself but also because it is a job which does not lend itself to neat, agreeable systems. Even the names of California's mountains—supposedly the most basic facts about them—can be confusing.

The U.S. Geological Survey (USGS) in one computerized listing of the state's mountains, recognizes three Mount Lewises, four Mount Hoffmans, six Eagle Peaks, seven Lookout Mountains, eleven Round Mountains, fourteen Bald Mountains, and sixteen Black Mountains. There are Red Buttes, Red Cinders, Red Cinder Cones, Red Cones, Red Hills, Red Mountains, Red Peaks, Red Rocks, and Red Tops, more than thirty "Reds" in all.

There is only one Mt. Whitney in California, but that name had to migrate from peak to peak as different mountains were acclaimed the state's tallest. Locals and old-timers cling affectionately and tenaciously to the earlier names of other peaks which, for various reasons, have been changed. And cartographers more than once have mistakenly labeled their maps of California, only to see their mistakes gain wide acceptance and eventually the official stamp of approval.

Obviously, then, agreement on the "facts" is less than unanimous because there is so much about California mountains that invites disagreement. But there is a second reason why finality about these mountains is elusive. The mountains themselves are simply not final. They are not finished. California's mountains are incessantly moving, growing, and eroding.

Even if every peak in the state were accurately measured tomorrow, many of those measurements would be outdated before they could be printed. Topographic maps and quadrangles are revised only infrequently, and it takes years, even decades, before new or corrected information such as peak

Sanford Lake, in the northern Sierra Nevada, is a scenic example of the thousands of lakes found throughout the mountains of California.
JOHN R. BOEHMKE

names or elevation figures can be included. Within that time, mountains may have risen or fallen several inches—if earthquakes or eruptions have not raised or lowered them many feet.

Similarly, the vegetation and wildlife of a mountain can change as quickly as fire can come and go. Landslides alter slopes or dam streams, creating lakes which become marshes which become meadows which become forests.

New highways can inch their precarious way along the sides of mountains and new subdivisions or resorts materialize almost overnight. Old highways and towns disappear.

In light of the scope and nature of California mountains, it is understandable—but still surprising—that *California Mountain Ranges* is the first book of its kind to embrace all the mountain regions of California. Selected ranges, especially the Sierra Nevada, have been the focus of book after book, but the effort to include every range in the state in one attractive, informative volume is for the most part untried.

Arranging *California Mountain Ranges* was not easy. It seemed inappropriate, in a book so rich in photography, to distinguish between mountain regions strictly on the basis of geology, since those distinctions are often quite technical and invisible to everyone but geologists.

Yet California's mountain ranges *were* created at different times, of different materials, and by different processes, and it seemed unnecessary to arrange the state's mountains strictly according to their location. Mountains all along the coast have much in common; so do the Sierra Nevada and Klamath ranges; so do the desert and Great Basin ranges, from California's northern to southern border.

Nevertheless, *California Mountain Ranges* explores the state's diverse mountains as consistently as possible from north to south.

There seems to be a consensus among Californians that all the state's mountains can be included

Miners played a major role in developing California's mountains. But now much of their work sits idle, serving only as reminders of a glorious and colorful era. Here, for example, are the historic ruins of the Kennedy Mine near Jackson, once the deepest mine in the United States. ED COOPER

in one of the following regions—Klamath Ranges; Cascade Range; Sierra Nevada; North Coast Ranges; South Coast Ranges; Transverse Ranges and the Tehachapis; Peninsular Ranges; or Basin Ranges.

This arrangement has general, but not universal, support. Some readers may point out, correctly, that the Tehachapis are geologically the southern extension of the Sierra Nevada. Others will point out, again correctly, that neither the desert ranges of southern California nor the Modoc Plateau ranges of northern California are technically part of the North American Basin-and-Range province.

And it will be unusual if the dividing lines between regions—between the Klamath and North Coast ranges, for example, or between the South Coast and Transverse ranges—do not spawn some disagreement.

Add to these topics of probable argument the certainty that some identifiable mountain range, somewhere in California, has been overlooked. *California Mountain Ranges* includes more than one hundred separate mountain ranges among its eight mountain regions. These ranges were selected largely on the basis of USGS maps. But not included under their own names here are mountain formations not officially designated as ranges, such as the Purisima Hills and Oak Ridge. Also not included are segments of official ranges which, even though considered by local residents to be distinct ranges, are not recognized as such.

Despite the unavoidable pitfalls of any scheme of organization, however, California has long deserved a book which portrays the state's mountains as what they are—each a fascinating part of the whole state, affecting the climate, commerce, agriculture, and recreation of the whole state.

The prominent, monolithic dome of Moro Rock (right) in Sequoia National Park (not to be confused with Morro Rock on the coast near San Luis Obispo) vividly illustrates the effects of exfoliation as clearly as does Yosemite's Half Dome. Exfoliation occurs when layers of granite peel away, perhaps because of alternate freezing and thawing in cracks in the rock.
TOM ALGIRE

The Sierra Nevada's Mt. Williamson (far right), seen here from Shepherd Pass, is not only California's second-highest peak but also one of the most massive, overshadowing all its neighboring peaks and visible from U.S. 395 for fifty miles. DAVID MUENCH

Mountains before names

Of all the stories told of the genesis of California's mountains, perhaps none are as intriguing as those told by geologists. Geology, of course, was not the first explanation to describe those ancient births in terms of immense conflicts and violence. Primitive man had always sensed that much. Geology does, however, narrate the most verifiable story to date—even if it, too, is filled with gaps and erosion and no small amount of conflict.

Imagine that the earth has a huge liquid center, incomprehensibly hot, composed of melted rock. Imagine further that this center is covered by a crust of hardened rock hundreds of miles thick, formed by melted rock which has cooled. Then imagine that this surrounding crust is not one evenly distributed layer, but rather is broken into gigantic plates as big as continents or ocean floors, much as mud cracks and breaks into chunks as it dries. Finally, imagine one thing more—that unlike chunks of dried mud, these massive plates of earth crust move in relation to each other, slowly churning above the fiery liquid center of the earth as if it were boiling.

This is how most geologists unfold the successive rises and falls of California mountains. There have been generations of these mountains, older ones giving way to younger ones which in turn disappeared. But it is the California mountains gathering rain and challenging road builders today which are of most interest.

Millions of years ago, as present-day California mountain ranges were beginning to emerge, the Pacific coastline of North America was far inland. Then something changed. Two huge plates of the earth's crust, the North American plate and the Pacific plate, began to grind against each other, and eventually the Pacific plate with all its seafloor rock began sliding underneath—or, more technically, subducting—the North American plate. It was this

The awesome 2,000-foot-high west face of North Palisade (14,242 feet) in the rugged backcountry of Kings Canyon National Park (left) is also a display of intrusive dikes and sills, the white stripes formed when molten rock was injected into cracks and joints in the main body of granite.
EUGENE FISHER

Volcanic deposits colored by mineral pigments (right) have earned these mountains in Death Valley National Monument an especially apt name—Artists Palette. Even the composition of some of the pigments is still unknown. Iron oxides, for example, may produce shades of violet, yellow, red, brown, and black, while green may be caused either by copper or mica. RENE PAULI

subduction which, in four different ways, formed the California landscape seen today.

First, as the Pacific plate was forced beneath the North American plate, it was also forced deeper below the earth's surface and closer to its liquid center, where it began to remelt. The remelting rock, however, brought something new into the fire—oxygen, gathered in the form of rust and other oxides. As this edge of the Pacific plate remelted, super-heated gases were released that exerted tremendous pressure, melting their way upward through the crust and venting themselves in towering chains of vocanoes.

Subduction of the continental plates was not continuous. In the last few million years, for example, subduction and volcanism resumed after a long period of inactivity, giving birth to the young Cascades, a string of volcanoes stretching from northern California all the way through Oregon and Washington.

Second, in what is now eastern California, a huge mass of molten rock was slowly rising toward the surface, cooling and hardening into granite before it broke through the crust. This block of underground granite would eventually become the Sierra Nevada, the largest continuous block of granite on earth. The young, still-growing Sierra Nevada was once submerged beneath erupting volcanoes.

Third, the North American plate was scraping off the uppermost surface of the subducting Pacific plate much as a snowplow scrapes the icy mountain roads of the Sierra Nevada, piling up great sheets and mounds of rubble. This seafloor rubble was piling in heaps farther and farther west, just above the northwest-southeast trench where the one plate ground beneath the other. Like an accordion, these heaps—which would become California's coastal mountains—rose one after another, steadily westward, as more and more seafloor was sheared off underneath.

Finally, with such titanic grinding between plates of the earth's crust, it's not surprising that cracks at the edges of contact occurred along the North American continent. The most famous of these, of course, is the San Andreas fault, essentially a network of cracks extending from southeast California and through the San Bernardino and San Gabriel mountains, then through San Francisco, and beneath the Pacific Ocean west of Cape Mendocino. The Pacific plate, diving beneath the North American plate in a northeastward direction, had already been buckling mountains inland. Now, it began to push or piggyback the broken sliver of California west of the faults, pushing that piece of California northward a few more inches every year. Land now at Point Reyes seems to have been torn and separated from the Sierra Nevada more than two hundred miles to the south.

And just east of Los Angeles, paralleling a bend

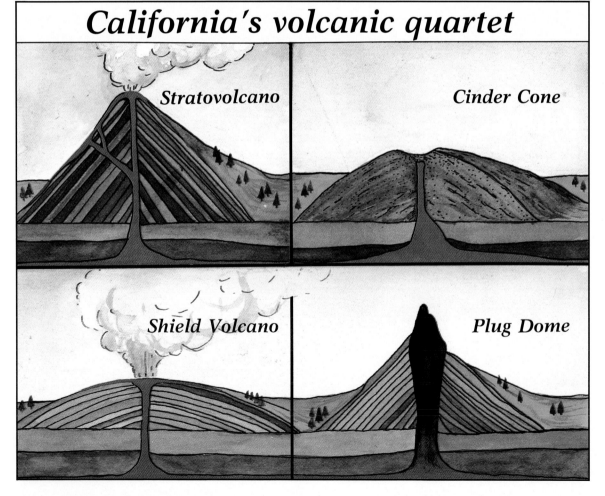

California's volcanic quartet

Stratovolcano

Cinder Cone

Shield Volcano

Plug Dome

in the San Andreas Fault, the predominant northwest-southeast trend of the Coast Ranges, scraped from the ocean floor, is suddenly twisted counterclockwise in a crimp which gives the Transverse Ranges the only sustained east-west trend in the state.

There may have been other fractures and movements, too. According to geologists, there has been a sixty-mile separation of the Sierra Nevada from the cluster of ranges known collectively as the Klamath Ranges, in northwestern California. Rocks of the two mountain ranges are very similar—the cores of the Trinity Alps are practically identical to those of the Sierra, for example, and both the western Sierra and the Marble Mountains of northwest California contain a distinctive type of marble. In fact, the only marble caves in California are found in the Marble Mountains and in the central and southern Sierra, leading geologists to speculate that the two ranges may have once been one.

Another major crack in the North American plate, the northeast-southwest-trending Garlock Fault, seems to have developed farther south in California, influenced by movements along the San Andreas Fault. Between Madera on the west side of the Sierra and Mono Lake on the east side, the range makes a pronounced bend south. Here, south of Yosemite, the North Fork of the San Joaquin River flows west through a deep canyon between Mt. Ritter and Banner Peak after draining the eastern slopes of the area's highest peaks. In other words, the real backbone of the Sierra Nevada is split by flowing water. Geologists believe the block of Sierra Nevada granite may be cracked here where it bends southward.

(Interestingly, since the crest of a mountain range is an imaginary dividing line determined not by elevation but by runoff waters, the crest of the Sierra Nevada here is forced by definition and by the Middle Fork of the San Joaquin River to follow lower peaks to the east.)

Such are the stories told by geologists. Like other

A lone climber (left) is dwarfed by Middle Palisade Glacier in Kings Canyon National Park. Today, all of the glaciers in the Sierra Nevada have a combined area of less than 20 square miles. Until about 20,000 years ago, however, glaciers covered all but the tallest Sierra peaks—an area 300 miles long, 30 miles wide, and in places, more than a mile deep. JEFF GNASS

Glacial polish (below) spreads like patches of ice across this slope in the Hoover Wilderness of the Sierra Nevada. Finely ground rock imbedded in or caught beneath moving glacial ice has polished the underlying rock until it shines, and the luster may last for centuries. CARR CLIFTON

stories, they describe what no one saw yesterday in order to explain what everyone can see today. The collision of plates of the earth's crust, for instance, helps explain why the Sierra are much steeper to the east than to the west. As a huge block of granite extending deep beneath the earth's surface, the Sierras have been tilted upward slightly at their southeastern edge like a four hundred-mile-long brick, forced by the pressure of the Pacific plate against the edge of the continent and by its grinding underneath. It may even be that the deep San Andreas Fault is the western, submerged edge of the Sierra "brick" and the counterpart to its steep eastern face.

The locations of volcanoes, too, make sense in these geologic stories of *plate tectonics*, where one plate of earth crust subducts another. As the Pacific plate angles deeper beneath the North American plate, escaping gases and the resultant volcanoes seem to mark the distance inland at which the subducting plate has plunged deep enough to remelt. Consequently, a chain of volcanoes paralleling the coastline, just as the Cascades do all the way into Canada, should be no surprise.

But why, then, is there not today (as there was long ago) a similar chain of volcanoes among or just west of the Sierra, also paralleling the coastline?

As a massive, rectangular brick partially buried in the earth, the Sierras *may* have acted as a plug to those escaping gases. In fact, the only major volcano in the Sierra, Mammoth Mountain (which still steams occasionally), is located at that one spot where the backbone (if not the crest) of the range is breached by the San Joaquin River—the theoretical crack in the Sierra brick, through which volcanic gases might be seeping.

In explaining the jumble of California's Coast Ranges, geologists find the stories of colliding plates most helpful of all. Without such stories, they were unable to explain, from the confusing mishmash of ocean sediment that comprised these mountains, how such mountains came to be and why the rocks here are progressively younger toward the ocean. By imagining the lower Pacific plate catching and dragging and skipping against the upper North American plate, geologists can describe how some layers of rock exposed along Coast Range highways are upside down, or separated by radically different rocks, or more frequently pulverized beyond recognition.

They can explain, too, why the Coast Ranges are some of the most erosive formations in the world. Water is saved the necessity of first crumbling these mountains. The major river of the North Coast Ranges, the Eel, carries one of the highest sediment loads of any river on earth, fifteen times that of the Mississippi, and is eroding these mountains at a rate of up to eighty inches per thousand years. (The Sierra Nevada, by contrast, is only surrendering about one inch to its rivers every thousand years.) Similarly, the notorious seaward-slanting slopes of the South Coast Ranges are eroded by frequent landslides.

Like most stories, those of geologists compress

A hanging valley is born

(1) Some of the most spectacular waterfalls in California plunge over hanging valleys, created by massive glaciers. Long before those glaciers appeared, rivers and tributaries had cut gentle V-shaped valleys in the mountains.

(2) Later those rivers and tributaries became glaciers, moving ice which scoured out U-shaped valleys and sheared off mountainsides. The valleys of larger rivers were gouged more deeply than those of smaller tributaries.

(3) When those glaciers receded, tributary valleys had become hanging valleys. The harder the underlying rock, the more resistant it was to further cutting by a prodigal tributary—and the longer the lifespan of the hanging valley.

Grinding away: Subduction and California's mountains

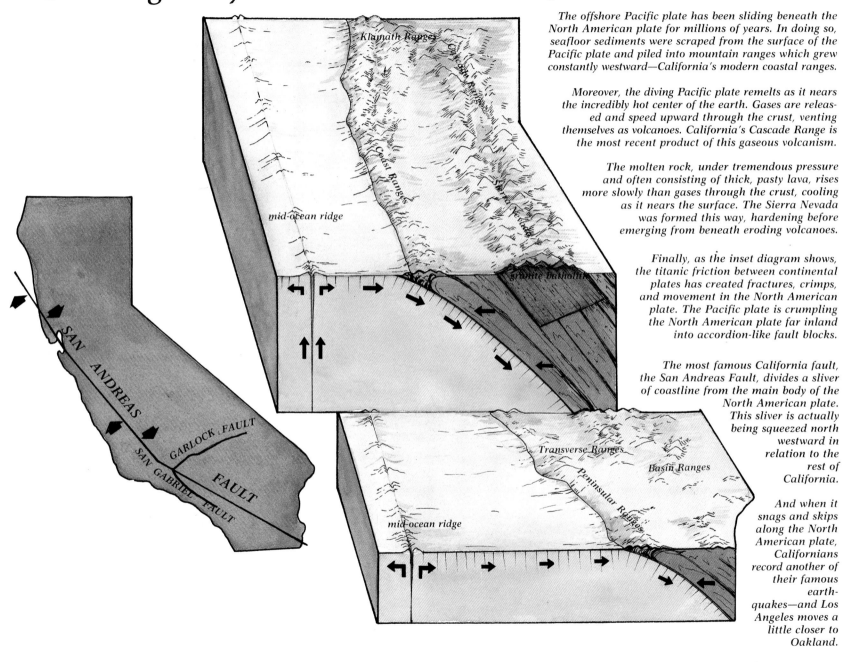

The offshore Pacific plate has been sliding beneath the North American plate for millions of years. In doing so, seafloor sediments were scraped from the surface of the Pacific plate and piled into mountain ranges which grew constantly westward—California's modern coastal ranges.

Moreover, the diving Pacific plate remelts as it nears the incredibly hot center of the earth. Gases are released and speed upward through the crust, venting themselves as volcanoes. California's Cascade Range is the most recent product of this gaseous volcanism.

The molten rock, under tremendous pressure and often consisting of thick, pasty lava, rises more slowly than gases through the crust, cooling as it nears the surface. The Sierra Nevada was formed this way, hardening before emerging from beneath eroding volcanoes.

Finally, as the inset diagram shows, the titanic friction between continental plates has created fractures, crimps, and movement in the North American plate. The Pacific plate is crumpling the North American plate far inland into accordion-like fault blocks.

The most famous California fault, the San Andreas Fault, divides a sliver of coastline from the main body of the North American plate. This sliver is actually being squeezed north westward in relation to the rest of California.

And when it snags and skips along the North American plate, Californians record another of their famous earthquakes—and Los Angeles moves a little closer to Oakland.

time—hundreds of millions of years into a few sentences. But there is ample evidence that, ever so slowly, the story of plate tectonics goes on. And often dramatically. The San Francisco earthquake of 1906, at the break between the North and South Coast ranges, resulted in a horizontal movement along the San Andreas Fault of twenty-one feet. In 1914 and for several years afterward, Mt. Lassen erupted and altered the landscape of the southern Cascades. The San Fernando earthquake of 1971 raised the San Gabriel Mountains in the Transverse Ranges some six feet. And on a smaller scale, scores of mudslides every year alter the terrain of California mountains in a matter of seconds.

Birth, of course, was not the end of the story for California's mountain ranges. The highest Sierra, Klamath, and Cascade peaks were gouged by ice.

Glaciers thousands of feet thick in the southern Sierra cut the highest and most breathtaking waterfalls on the continent and made the Sierra one of the most glaciated mountain ranges in the world. The rivers of ice carved Yosemite, Hetch Hetchy, Tenaya, and other stream valleys into broad troughs. Smaller glaciers sculpted peaks throughout the Klamath Ranges, particularly the Trinity Alps; the Yolla Bolly Mountains, which extend into the North Coast Ranges; the Cascades, especially Mt. Shasta, Lassen Peak, and Mt. Hoffman; the White Mountains; and even as far south as San Gorgonio Mountain in the Transverse Ranges.

As glaciers advanced and retreated over the course of centuries, they left behind moraines, ridges of rubble marking the sides (lateral moraines) and leading edges (terminal moraines) of glaciers. They also deposited erratics, huge boulders which today dot the mountain landscape in flat, open areas where they seem strangely out of place.

Only about sixty glaciers, most of them tiny, remain in the Sierra Nevada, almost all above 10,500 feet elevation. They have a combined area of less than twenty miles. The only California glaciers found outside of the Sierra are on the slopes of Mt. Shasta in the Cascades—five of them, equally small.

Some glaciers actually seem to be growing, however, thanks to a twenty-year cooling trend. Heavy snowpack in 1977-1978, for example, became "firn" by surviving the following summer and then, because of early snows in autumn 1978, became new glacial ice.

Other forces, too, shaped the mountains. Sediment was carried in streams down the long, gentle western slopes of the Sierra, where it kept the rugged feet of the mountains covered with rolling foothills. Heavier precipitation in the Klamaths increased runoff and cut deep V-shaped valleys. To the south, the Basin Ranges were sandblasted by desert winds and, despite less rainfall, were eroded more quickly by water because of their lack of vegetation. The Coast Ranges, rising more than an inch a year in places, created new marine terraces like stairsteps while pounding waves cut caves, arches, and precipitous cliffs.

There was a relatively new force, too, affecting the mountains—life.

Cinder Cone, in the northeast corner of Lassen Volcanic National Park, is an amazingly symmetrical example of one type of volcano by the same name. Rising 600 feet above the surrounding flatlands, Cinder Cone was formed when exploded volcanic debris rained down near its vent. Like typical cinder cones, it has a circular base; steep, regular slopes; and lava streams issuing from the base of the cone. JEFF GNASS

Erosion has dramatically furrowed volcanic ash at one of the two Ubehebe Craters in Death Valley National Monument, and the Last Chance Range rises in the background. These craters were formed by explosive eruptions and are ringed with volcanic debris. Unlike blowout craters in wetter areas (such as the Inyo Craters on the east side of the Sierra Nevada), however, the Ubehebe Craters have not formed lakes. TOM BEAN

Breccia—rock consisting of sharp fragments cemented or embedded in fine-grained clay or sand—creates a natural mosaic on the walls of Titus Canyon in the Grapevine Mountains. TOM BEAN

The faceted basalt columns of Devil's Postpile National Monument near Mammoth Lakes (left) are as regularly patterned as any in the world. The six-sided column—formed when cooling liquid rock was split by vertical joints—is nature's most efficient geometric shape. MICHAEL S. SAMPLE

Seen from this perspective (bottom left), the columns of the Devil's Postpile more closely resemble the massive lava flow which originated several miles to the southeast near Mammoth Mountain. Where lava cooled on level ground, such as in lakes or pools, the resulting columns are almost perfectly vertical. Where it flowed and cooled over uneven ground, the columns are twisted and bent like these. MICHAEL S. SAMPLE

The tops of these same basalt columns (bottom right), sheared off and cleanly polished by glaciers, form a natural tile-floor pattern. MICHAEL S. SAMPLE

The crest of the Sierra Nevada (opposite page) is framed by this eroded rock arch in boulder-littered Owens Valley. DAVID MUENCH

Mountain flora and fauna:

Mountains of life

California's mountains are alive.

The fascinating, incredibly diverse vegetation of California's mountains reflects broad patterns of precipitation. Mountain forests cover a fifth of the state, from one end to the other, which is as much area as all its agricultural land combined. The state flower, the California poppy, flourishes on gentle foothills throughout the state. Manzanita, with its striking oily-reddish bark, waxy leaves, and red berries thrives in every section of the state, as do hybridized oaks. Other plants, however, are much more restricted in range.

The insect-eating California pitcher plant is confined to the Klamath Ranges and the northern Sierra. The weeping spruce is found in California only in the Klamath Ranges. Santa Lucia firs grow only in the South Coast Ranges, restricted specifically to the Santa Lucia Range. Coulter pines, bearers of the world's heaviest cones (some as heavy as ten pounds), are limited to the South Coast, Transverse, and Peninsular ranges. Tanoaks, extensively harvested for their tannic acids until synthetic substitutes diminished the value of the trees to the leather industry, are Coast Ranges trees, although scattered stands remain in the Mount Shasta area and the northern Sierra. Bristlecone pines, among the earth's oldest living organisms (one reaching 4,600 years), are found on the highest, cruellest peaks of the Basin Range mountains to the east of the Sierra. Manzanita's larger cousin, the madrone tree, intermingles with northern forests only. And as many as nine species of cypress live only in isolated pockets, some even in single groves.

The twin princes of California vegetation are the coastal redwood and the giant sequoia. Before California's Gold Rush, coastal redwoods (which rarely grow at elevations higher than 3,000 feet) spread in a consistent band thirty miles wide and about 450 miles long, from Oregon south to the Santa Lucia Mountains. After intensive lumbering, less than 70,000 acres of virgin redwood forest remain today, 50,000 acres of that protected in state and federal parks lush with sword ferns and vine maple. Yet despite such extensive cutting, there may well be more trees of this species living today—although younger and smaller—than existed before white men cut the first one. Every time a coastal redwood is cut, it sends up four, five, six or more new sprouts which, if allowed to grow, can each become a mature tree. Moreover, coastal

A female Costa's hummingbird (left) draws nectar from delphinium flowers in the Trinity Alps.
DAVID CAVAGNARO

The deeply furrowed trunks (right) of the Big Trees, giant sequoias seem to materialize from the mist in Unnamed Grove, Sequoia National Park. These trees, the largest of all living things, rely on fire to flourish. Their thick, nonresinous bark contains large amounts of fire-retarding tannin, and their lower branches quickly die from lack of sunlight, keeping the trees' foliage out of reach of flames. DAVID MUENCH

redwoods have been transplanted as commercial trees, most significantly to New Zealand half a century ago, and hundreds of thousands of acres of these giants now thrive outside their native home.

The giant sequoia, the largest living thing on earth, does not have the regenerative capability of its coastal relative, and may be in greater danger. Limited in range to the western Sierra, it needs periodic fires to trigger germination of its tiny seeds (91,000 to the pound) and to clear the ground of choking undergrowth. Fortunately, the giant sequoia has also been less attractive to timber cutters—not as durable as the wood of the coastal redwood, the giant sequoia also shatters easily when felled, and was never logged extensively for anything other than fence posts.

Giant sequoias, too, have been carried by man far beyond California—but not as commercial lumber like their coastal cousins. They were planted as ornamentals in England before the Civil War, and avenues there are lined with the towering trees. They grow in Switzerland, France, Germany, Spain, and even Yugoslavia.

Vegetation in California's mountains reflects other, more localized influences as well as precipitation. The direction a slope faces—whether north or south—has a tremendous impact upon vegetation, determining as it does the amount of sunlight and evaporation affecting plant life. The type of soil in a particular area is crucial, too. Particularly striking effects of soil differences on vegetation are evident in chaotic formations such as the Coast Ranges. Depth of soil determines vegetation, as do persistent winds, drainage characteristics, and natural disruptions such as fires, floods, landslides, volcanic activity, and avalanches.

Altitude, though, with its related temperatures and precipitation, is the key to understanding

California's first mountain men

Among the species native to California mountains was man. As early as thirty thousand years ago, Californians began a tradition of barbecuing a dwarf mammoth. For the most part, these aboriginal inhabitants lived a Stone Age existence, with no system of writing and no knowledge of the wheel. Best estimates put the relatively stable population of California Indians at about 300,000, concentrated along the foothills of the Coast Ranges, on the western slopes of the Sierras, and in the Central Valley.

The first Californians were mainly hunters, fishers, and gatherers. Dogs were their only domesticated animals, and intoxicatingly strong tobacco their only cultivated crop. Densities of human beings here in this abundant land were four times greater than anywhere else in North America, and were greater than any other nonagricultural population in the world.

Yet living as they did among mountains—Nature's fences—in small groups and without the adversity so closely associated with highly developed cultures (Miwoks died more often of tooth infections than in wars), California's Indians remained surprisingly divided despite their numbers. They spoke six different primary languages, more than eighty mutually unintelligible tongues, and more than three hundred dialects—a diversity equivalent to that of all of Europe.

In fact, practically the only contact these small families of California Indians had with each other resulted from trading skins for baskets, shells for acorns, straight arrow shafts for obsidian arrowpoints, and all of these for salt. Most commodities were traded between neighbors, but long-distance trade routes were also developed, foreshadowing almost exactly California's present-day interstate highway system and discovering and utilizing, long before white men, crossings of the Sierra such as Mono Pass, Kearsarge Pass, and Walker Pass.

These rock drawings in the Coso Mountains in the Basin Ranges typify those left by California's early residents. MARGARET MALM/NATURE PIX

They make the weather

Water determines life in California, and mountains determine water. Because the temperature of the atmosphere drops more than one degree Fahrenheit with every increase of 300 feet, air gets colder as it ascends mountain slopes. Conversely, air descending mountain slopes is compressed and thus heated at approximately the same rate.

By itself, this warming and cooling of air would have little effect on California were it not for the tremendous amounts of moisture often contained in that air, moisture absorbed from the Pacific Ocean. California averages about 200 million acre-feet of precipitation each year, enough to cover every inch of the state nearly two feet deep in water.

Elevation and its resulting effect, rainshadow, are the chief causes of vastly different rainfall amounts within comparatively small areas. For example, Trinidad, in the North Coast Ranges, is only two hundred feet higher than Eureka, twenty miles south, but averages twice as much rainfall. Santa Cruz, on the coast, averages 24 inches of rain a year while San Jose, 25 miles beyond the first South Coast Range ridge, averages 13 inches.

Warm air can hold more moisture than cold air, and as air is cooled, it reaches a dew point at which humidity (water vapor) begins to condense. Since masses of air must rise to cross mountains, they cool and begin to drop their moisture. The higher they rise, the cooler they become, and the more of their moisture they lose as precipitation. If the mountains are high enough, an air mass may lose virtually all of its moisture. In southern California, for instance, where the air typically carries less moisture to begin with, precipitation from some air masses may end as low as 5,500 feet, after which the mountains can wring no more water. In fact, some air masses may be so dry by the time they

A lightning storm lights up the Cascade Range in northern California. CARR CLIFTON

cross a ridge or range of mountains that they actually evaporate water from air on the other side as they descend and warm, lowering the humidity.

This rainshadow effect can be caused by a single peak—Mt. Tamalpais just north of San Francisco, for example, creates its own rainshadow. And the effect may persist far inland. Despite the fact that air is generally drier in southern California, the northern Sierra Nevada are not substantially wetter than the central or southern Sierra. Why? Because the North Coast Ranges are generally higher and broader than the South Coast Ranges, and thus wring more water from passing clouds.

Just as importantly for Sierra rainfall and

snowfall, moist ocean air gushes through gaps in mountain barriers (such as the San Francisco Bay) and mingles in the Central Valley before rising again over the towering Sierra, which, in turn, creates its own long rainshadow.

Because the Coast Ranges rarely drain all the moisture from passing air; because infusions of quite moist air often occur in the Central Valley; and because the Sierra are so much higher than the mountains to the west and are thus more able to cool air coming from that direction, the western slopes of the Sierra, especially between elevations of 2,000 and 9,000 feet, receive substantial amounts of rain and snow. Lower mountains to the north and south of the Sierra, on the other hand, are quite arid in comparison.

vegetation in a mountainous state such as California. San Gorgonio Mountain, north of Palm Springs in the Transverse Ranges, provides vivid evidence of that importance. A hiker who left Interstate 10 at San Gorgonio Pass (1,500 feet) and climbed to the mountain's peak (11,502 feet) would see the same evolution of vegetation, from desert cactus to wildflowers growing in bare rock and ice, that he would encounter on a flatland journey from Mexico to arctic Alaska.

Particular communities of plants exist in particular climates, and when these climates are determined by altitude rather than by latitude, drainage, soil quality, direction of slope, or traumatic disruptions, botanists speak of *vegetation zones*. Of course botanists, like geologists, are not inclined to agree with each other, and literally dozens of different zone classification systems have taken root, many of them quite intricate and vast. Common among all classifications of vegetation habitats, however, is a ready admission that adjacent zones overlap, sometimes inextricably; that zone elevations differ on the windward and leeward slopes of mountains; and that not every plant typical of a particular zone will actually inhabit that zone throughout the state. Lodgepole pines, for instance, are rarely found in California west of the Sierra and Douglas firs are rare south of the Santa Cruz Mountains (although closely related big-cone Douglas firs are found in the mountains of southern California).

One of the most useful—although greatly simplified—of these schemes divides the vegetation of western North America into six major zones, named for the geographical areas where each plant community is most prevalent. These include (1) the Lower Sonoran zone (500 feet and below), characterized mainly by cactus and other desert plants; (2) the Upper Sonoran zone (500-5,000 feet), characterized by dense chaparral, currants, ceanothus, clusters of oaks among grasslands, and digger pines; (3) the Transition zone (3,000-8,000 feet), characterized by yellow (ponderosa) pines, denser stands of oaks, and sometimes white firs, sycamores, willows, cottonwoods, and big-leaf maples; (4) the Canadian zone (6,000-10,000 feet), typified by forests of lodgepole pines and red firs, Douglas firs, and incense cedars; (5) the Hudsonian zone, just below timberline, signalled by the appearance of heather and whitebark pine; and (6) the Arctic-Alpine zone, above timberline, where a smattering of thick, hardy, ground-hugging plants eke out a living despite thin soils, harshly cold semi-permanent winds, and intense solar radiation.

The giant sequoias provide an important insight into the concept of vegetation zones. At one end of their distribution, in the lower, northern Sierra, these Big Trees grow at elevations close to 2,700 feet, mainly on south-facing slopes. The further south they grow, however, the higher in elevation they grow, compensating for warmer temperatures and drier conditions by seeking out higher slopes. At the opposite end of their distribution, in the higher, southern Sierra, they grow at elevations as high as 8,800 feet, usually on north-facing slopes.

Similarly, the Arctic-Alpine vegetation zone slowly descends from the highest peaks in Mexico

Vegetation zones in the mountains

ARCTIC ALPINE
above timberline
(hardy ground-hugging plants)

HUDSONIAN
just below timberline
(heather, whitebark pine)

CANADIAN
6,000-10,000
(lodgepole pine, red fir, Douglas fir, incense cedar)

TRANSITION
3,000-8,000
(Ponderosa pine, cottonwood, oak, maple, willow, sycamore)

UPPER SONORAN
500-5,000
(chaparral, currant, digger pine)

LOWER SONORAN
below 500
(cactus, desert plants)

Wringing the clouds: Rainshadow patterns in California

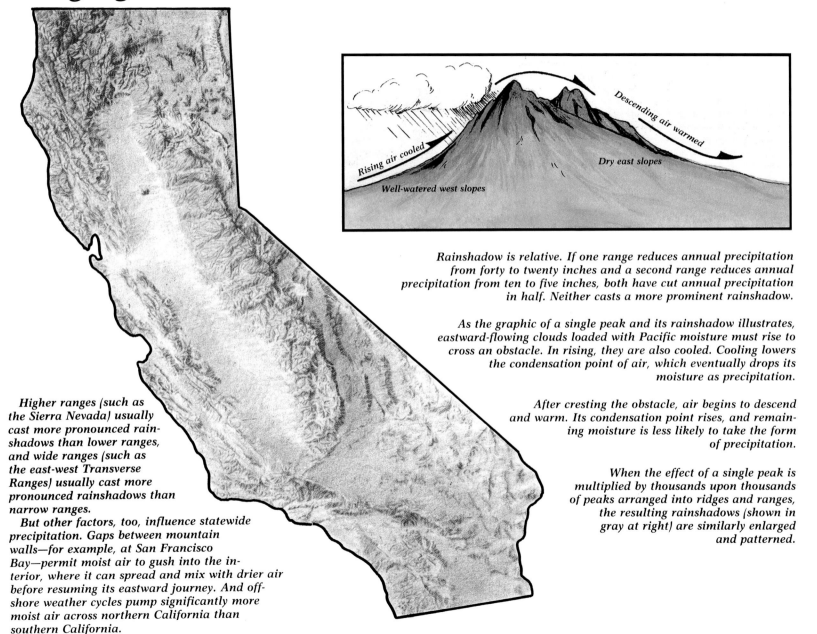

Rising air cooled

Well-watered west slopes

Descending air warmed

Dry east slopes

Rainshadow is relative. If one range reduces annual precipitation from forty to twenty inches and a second range reduces annual precipitation from ten to five inches, both have cut annual precipitation in half. Neither casts a more prominent rainshadow.

As the graphic of a single peak and its rainshadow illustrates, eastward-flowing clouds loaded with Pacific moisture must rise to cross an obstacle. In rising, they are also cooled. Cooling lowers the condensation point of air, which eventually drops its moisture as precipitation.

After cresting the obstacle, air begins to descend and warm. Its condensation point rises, and remaining moisture is less likely to take the form of precipitation.

When the effect of a single peak is multiplied by thousands upon thousands of peaks arranged into ridges and ranges, the resulting rainshadows (shown in gray at right) are similarly enlarged and patterned.

Higher ranges (such as the Sierra Nevada) usually cast more pronounced rainshadows than lower ranges, and wide ranges (such as the east-west Transverse Ranges) usually cast more pronounced rainshadows than narrow ranges.

But other factors, too, influence statewide precipitation. Gaps between mountain walls—for example, at San Francisco Bay—permit moist air to gush into the interior, where it can spread and mix with drier air before resuming its eastward journey. And offshore weather cycles pump significantly more moist air across northern California than southern California.

until, in Alaska, it is found at sea level.

Inhabiting these various vegetation life zones are the animals of California's mountains, each beautiful and crafty in its own way. The acorn woodpecker, his red cap glimpsed mainly in the oak woodlands of the South Coast Ranges, drills holes in oak trees and hammers acorns tip-end first until they are flush with the bark, storing them for winter. Near fast-flowing mountain streams throughout northern California, the robin-sized water ouzel, forgetting it is a bird, closes trap doors over its nostrils, dives underwater, and walks upright along the streambed, clinging to stones until it loses its footing, at which time it proceeds to "fly" underwater, searching for aquatic insects.

In mountain chaparral, California quail digest plants which, in dry seasons, contain ingredients inhibiting brood production. And on the thermals of the South Coast and Transverse ranges soar the last of the world's rarest birds—California condors, with nine-foot wingspans, numbering fewer than thirty (and most of those in captivity) after once ranging from British Columbia to Mexico, from California to Texas and Florida.

As early as 1873, felony laws and the threat of prison sentences protected the majestic, overhunted Roosevelt elk, which today browse the open meadows of their North Coast Ranges home. Black bears plod through all of California's major mountain areas as far south as the Transverse Ranges. In the foothills of the Coast and Sierra ranges, ringtails (nicknamed "miners' cats" because so many were kept as pets by gold seekers) stalk wood rats which venture out from huge stick nests several feet high. Higher up, near timberline, tiny rabbit-like creatures called pikas gather grasses and spread them on rocks to dry like hay, then store the bundles for winter.

An estimated two thousand mountain lions, powerful enough when full-grown to kill a two-hundred-pound mule deer with a single bite, still

pad through the most remote canyons of mountain ranges throughout California, and several regions re-opened hunting seasons on the great cats in 1985. Also numbering in the hundreds, bighorn sheep scramble along rocks at the highest altitudes of the Transverse, Peninsular, and Basin ranges and southern Sierra. They are among California's most endangered species, despite the fact that the state halted shooting of the majestic animals in 1883. Few mountain climbers now ever see a string of bighorns which, having followed their mothers as lambs, continue as adults to follow a ewe single-file along game trails. Fewer mountain climbers still ever see the colossal clashes between rutting rams, which may butt heads at seventy miles an hour as many as forty times in one afternoon to establish dominance.

Some animals, such as the grizzly bear, have wholly disappeared from California's mountains. Others, such as martens, wolverines, and red foxes, are on the brink of disappearing. Yet, there are still other animals which appeared in these mountains only recently and have proliferated. Honey bees, introduced to North America from Europe, had spread throughout California before

the arrival of the first white explorers, who found Indians already gathering wild honey in the Coast Ranges and western Sierra. Wild boars of the Coast Ranges, introduced by the Spanish, weigh as much as six hundred pounds and are California's second-ranked big game animal, barely trailing mule deer in numbers killed by hunters.

Most feral burros thriving in the lower elevations of the Basin Ranges escaped from miners—little nostalgic consolation to ranchers of the region who are repeatedly awakened at night by the braying courtship of these wild asses visiting domesticated stock.

Beaver, native in the Cascade and Klamath ranges, were recently introduced into the Kern River region of the southern Sierra by park managers and adapted excessively well. In fact, they are now being killed off there after those same managers realized that beaver dams were keeping California's golden trout, once found nowhere but here, from spawning.

As the last source of California's undeveloped rivers and streams, the North Coast and Klamath ranges are home to some of the most spirited fish in the West. Steelhead, essentially seagoing rainbow trout, return via the free-flowing waters of these mountains as many as four times to spawn in their freshwater birthplaces. Yet, silt from logged mountainsides and proposals for water projects threaten even these waters. The Smith River, in fact, is the only river in California which has completely escaped damming, although long stretches of other rivers still flow uninterrupted.

Of course, literally thousands of other species, plant and animal, inhabit California's mountains, taking advantage of every life zone, every acre, and each other, too. Dramas of death and birth and life are continual here. So is tragedy and beauty. In fact, California's mountains are not primarily towering or majestic or formidable. More than anything else, California's mountains are lively.

A Joshua Tree (far left) basks in winter sunlight on Marble Mountain in Death Valley National Monument. Although associated with the blistering Basin Ranges and higher deserts, Joshua Trees actually need winter frost to develop properly and die when transplanted to milder climates. FRED HIRSCHMANN

A black bear (left) feeds in a mountainside meadow. Occasionally weighing more than three hundred pounds, black bears are commonly found throughout California's mountain regions except for the Peninsular and Basin ranges. JAN L. WASSINK

California poppies (bottom left), formerly thought exclusive to the Pacific slope, can now be found in large numbers here in the western Antelope Valley. Botanists believe a combination of low mountain passes, ranges of moderate elevation, and a relatively uniform climate permitted California poppies to "leak" eastward through the mountains. WILLIAM HELSEL

A wild burro and her colt (bottom, right) pause in the barren terrain near Death Valley. Although burros were introduced to North America as early as the sixteenth century, it was not until earlier this century—when motorized vehicles replaced them in cross-country travel and packing—that great numbers were set free. Burros compete with desert bighorn sheep for food, and the exotic burros have contributed to the sharp decline of the bighorn. Now, burros are being removed from some areas such as the Panamint Mountains. LINDA WEEKS

Insectivorous California pitcher plants (above) unfurl as spring snows melt along Swift Creek Trail in the Trinity Alps Wilderness. This intriguing species is confined to moist areas in southern Oregon, the Klamath Ranges, and the northern Sierra. LARRY ULRICH

Wildflowers blanket the Merced River Canyon (right), west of Yosemite Valley, with vibrant colors. WILLIAM NEILL

The twisted, magnificent oak near Monterey (middle right) is typical of the most common trees on the lower slopes of California's mountains. Approximately sixteen species of oak flourish in California. Because oaks hybridize easily, California's mountains are home to a bewildering variety of these trees, often making accurate identification impossible. DAVID MUENCH

Splotches of lichen as bright and colorful as splashes of paint decorate this rock formation in the White Mountains (far right). Rock lichens are more than decoration, however, paving the way for mosses, grasses, shrubs, and trees. The lichen release chemicals which speed the breakdown and erosion of rock into soil, and their decaying tissues often add the first organic material to that soil. RENE PAULI

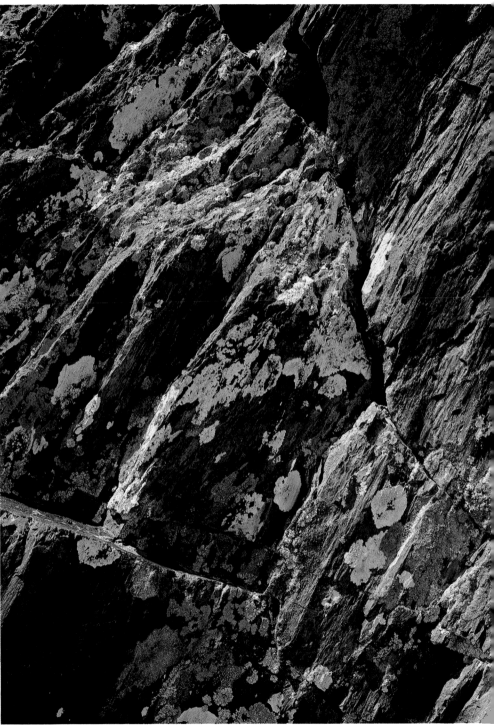

Since the days of legendary Norman Clyde, patriarch of California mountain climbers, the tools and techniques of peak baggers have undergone an amazing revolution. Clyde, credited with some 130 first ascents and more than a thousand climbs above 10,000 feet in California, often climbed alone, lugging ninety-pound packs which included guns, axes, cast-iron pots, cameras, fishing poles, and even books in Greek.

In the 1930s, climbers began relying on each other and on hardware—hemp rope; iron and later steel pitons pounded into cracks; expansion bolts drilled into solid granite. Today, however, "free" or "clean" climbing— no drilling, splitting, splintering, or altering of the rock—is made possible by high-tech equipment. High-friction climbing shoes have narrow, tapered toes and smooth, pliable, sticky soles. Modern ropes are cored with 70,000 tiny threads and sheathed with cut-resistant outer fibers. Spring-loaded devices, made of aluminum alloys with ten times more friction against rock than either iron or steel, can be wedged into tiny fractures without damaging the rock or endangering the climber. And special gymnastic chalk keeps fingers and palms impeccably dry.

Climbers in the Ten Lakes region of Yosemite National Park (opposite page, left) use a trusty compass and topographic map to find the best route. CHARLIE BORLAND

The daring rock climber slowly conquering "Angel Wings" (opposite page, right) is scaling the highest, steepest, and most spectacular rock wall in Sequoia National Park.
PETE COLE/THE STOCK SOLUTION

A mountain challenges climbers simply because it is a mountain, regardless of location. This rockclimber (left) has matched himself against sheer rock faces in the Little San Bernardino Mountains, Joshua Tree National Monument.
PATTY A. FURBUSH

Finally (below), the reward—the climber celebrates in the last rays of sunlight on the crest of Mt. Whitney. GEORGE WUERTHNER

The Klamath Ranges:
Out of California's way

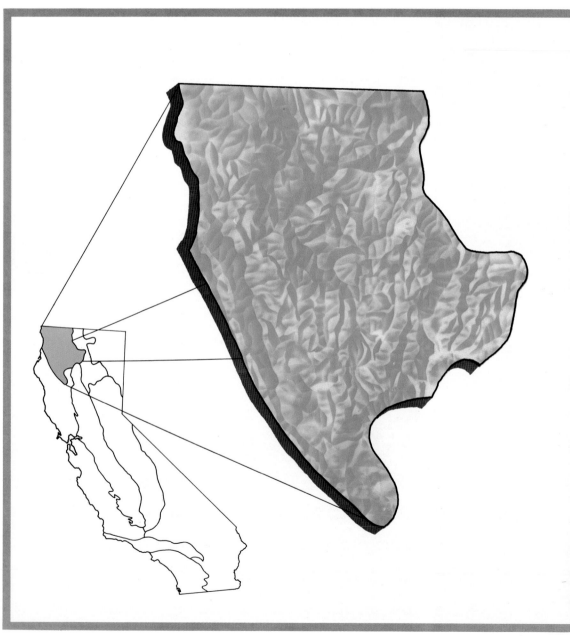

The isolated Klamath Ranges region, unlike the North Coast Ranges to its southwest, has several identifiable mountain ranges without a common trend. The Siskiyou Mountains north of the Klamath River, for example, arc roughly east to west, then north to south near their southern terminus. The Scott Bar, Marble, and Scott mountains stretch roughly northeast to southwest. The Trinity Mountains (partially separated from the Trinity Alps, highest peaks in the region, by Clair Engle Lake) run north-south, as do the northern Yolla Bollys. And the Salmon Mountains-Trinity Alps divide curves sharply from northwest to east.

The Klamath Ranges extend east from the northwestern corner of California to Interstate 5, where the jagged Castle Crags, more than 6,000 feet high, overlook the Sacramento Valley and the beginning of the Cascades to the east; and south from the Oregon border to the Sacramento Valley and South Fork Mountain, which separates the Klamath and North Coast ranges.

Five major rivers drain these mountains—the Smith, Klamath, Trinity, Scott, and Salmon rivers—creating the most dissected mountain landscape for its size in all of California. It is rugged and remote country, nearly 12,000 square miles (more than 7 million acres) penetrated by a single major highway, U.S. 299, and two smaller state highways. Trails used by trappers, prospectors, and cattlemen are still the only access to vast tracts of land—not counting thousands of miles of logging roads.

Not a single city is located within these mountains, and towns (none with populations over 4,000) are widely scattered. Population in the region averages about five people per square mile—almost as sparse as the state of Wyoming. Three national forests—Six Rivers (1,118,000 acres), Klamath (1,671,000 acres), and Trinity (600,000 acres)—support significant populations of endangered species, including peregrine falcons and bald eagles.

For backpackers and campers who prefer their

Western azalea (left), with Bear Mountain shrouded by fog in the background, blooms amid the rugged beauty of the Siskiyou Mountains Wilderness in the Klamath Ranges. The fragrant western azalea is usually found at moist sites. LARRY ULRICH

Fall color drenches Canyon Creek in the Trinity Alps Wilderness (above), which originates from several alpine snowfields and tumbles southward for 17 miles through a remarkably straight canyon and into the Trinity River. Not only are the Trinity Alps often considered a miniature Sierra Nevada because of soaring, glaciated peaks and alpine lakes. They were also once a miniature Mother Lode, complete with gold towns linked by the famous Trinity Trail, an Indian path turned pioneer trail turned Gold Rush wagon road. California 299 now parallels that historic trail. LEO L. LARSON

outdoors lonely, these mountains have no equals. Nothing makes the night sky brighter than the dark, surrounding depths of these forests. The air is so clean that stars barely twinkle. Moonlit wisps of clouds, some skinny, some fat, float above regal Douglas firs in humble review, while winds ebb and flow in branches which squeak against each other like birds. A quarter moon, with its luminous back, slowly slides—like a bear—up one trunk at the horizon.

Starting near the coast, the mountain ranges of the Klamath complex rise from elevations averaging less than 2,000 feet to those averaging more than 7,000 feet in the South Fork, Salmon, and northern Yolla Bolly mountains. Individual peaks go much higher, however. Thompson Peak, for instance, on the Trinity-Salmon divide, reaches 9,002 feet above sea level; China Mountain at the north end of the Scott Mountains, 8,542 feet; and nearby Mt. Eddy, in the shadow of Mt. Shasta, 9,025 feet.

Extensive timber cutting occurs in the Klamath ranges. Approximately 85 percent of the timber crop is Douglas fir, but loggers also harvest sugar, Jeffrey, and ponderosa pines as well. Inaccessibility and wilderness status, however, have reduced timber cutting in the majority of the interior.

Nearly forty miles east of Crescent City, Boulder Peak (6,028 feet) offers a panoramic 360-degree view, sighting along the rugged backbone of the Siskiyou Mountains toward the Pacific Ocean. The High Siskiyous, as the highest, westernmost mountains of the range are called, culminate in glacier-gouged crests, the result (at these relatively low elevations) of bearing the brunt of Pacific storms moving over much lower ridges to the west. Preston Peak (7,309 feet) is by far the highest point in the range, but even much lower elevations are consistently buried by snow in the winter.

As one of the major timber-producing ranges of northern California, the Siskiyous were subjected to intense lumbering for many years. However, because they are steeper and more erosive than other Klamath ranges, rivers and streams that were once prime salmon and steelhead fisheries became loaded with silt, threatening clean gravel spawning grounds. The new Siskiyou Mountains Wilderness surrounding Preston Peak now prohibits logging on the higher mountains of the range.

Also facing the Siskiyous until recently was the prospect of strip mining. The Siskiyous are a major

Red kinnikinnick berries, formerly important to the survival of California's Indians, add an almost festive appearance to this mat of caribou moss. Also known as bearberry, the kinnikinnick produces berries throughout the year, including winter. Indians preferred to soak the dry berries in fish oil or pick them after they had been sweetened by the first frost. They used the leaves, too, for tea and later (after the arrival of white men), they dried and smoked them. LEO L. LARSON

source of extractable chromium and the only source of cobalt in the United States. Political and racial unrest in South Africa, the major U.S. supplier of these minerals, has intensified pressure to open the Siskiyous to strip mining, despite the possibility of leaching toxic chemicals into the Smith River, protected under the federal Wild and Scenic Rivers Act. But recently the U.S. Congress, in an atmosphere of soaring budget deficits and painful funding cuts, was unwilling to approve a $50 million strategic minerals subsidy backed by the Administration and considered essential to large-scale extraction of minerals in the Siskiyous. Proponents and opponents of such development agree, however, that the battle is far from over.

The Klamath River, the southern and eastern boundary of the Siskiyous, enters the Klamath ranges through steep canyon walls and smooth mountainsides sparsely vegetated with scrub oak. Flowing west from Interstate 5, it avoids symmetrical piles of smooth boulders, left there by gold dredges half a century ago, and loops around green meadows. Children at recess outside the yellow elementary school in Horse Creek yell to anglers floating the lazy river in dories. Local gardeners kick disgustedly at dense hedgerows of thorny vines, cursing the Tennessean who rode through these mountains in 1910, peddling young "Himalayan berries" for a dime a bundle. The introduced blackberries cover slopes and fences and kill trees, and seem impervious to chopping, digging, burning, and even goats.

Farther downstream, the mountains above the river become more rugged—too steep even for pack animals—and scars old and recent serve as reminders that these mountains can be dangerous. The 1964 storms which dumped more than twenty

Wedding Cake Mountain and Mt. Thompson (right) tower above the Salmon-Trinity Alps Primitive Area. Deep glacial canyons and huge boulders, often above 9,000 feet, characterize these spectacular mountains. ED COOPER

inches of rain in the Klamath and Eel basins in a few days erased towns from the landscape if not from subsequent maps. Where Cottage Grove is supposed to be, under the shadow of Dillon Mountain (4,679 feet), modern-day prospectors search for treasures with metal detectors, finding silver sugar bowls, stoves, and silverware among the rusted shells of automobiles. The town of Klamath, too, was washed away, and what was once its downtown is now a road that disappears into blackberry vines.

Huge spoon-shaped excavations are everywhere on these slopes of Douglas fir and sugar pine, fresh tell-tale wounds where whole ridges of earth and rock let go, often sliding to the far side of the river and altering its course.

To the southeast of the Siskiyous, the twenty-mile-long Scott Bar Mountains offer splendid views of the Marble and Salmon mountains from near Fort Jones, where Ulysses S. Grant became an AWOL soldier after failing to take command of the fort as assigned. South of the Siskiyous, on the Pacific Crest Trail, the bald ridge of solid white limestone that tops Marble Mountain overlooks the 214,000-acre Marble Mountain Wilderness, centered around the Sky High Lakes and Kings Castle (7,405 feet).

The Marble Mountains, aptly named in light of the distinctive marble core which may link them to the Sierra, are famous for their marble caves. Backpackers lug heavy spelunking equipment far into the wilderness to explore literally miles of deep caves, many never entered before.

And still farther south, the newly enlarged Salmon-Trinity Alps Wilderness includes nearly half a million acres of high, rugged ridges, deep glacial canyons, and numerous backpacking trails

Beside Devil's Punchbowl Creek in the proposed Siskiyou Mountains Wilderness, boulders are draped with western azalea. LARRY ULRICH

rising 3,000 feet in less than four miles.

The soaring, granite Trinity Alps, hidden from nearby Interstate 5 by lesser mountains, are strikingly similar to some of the Sierra's craggiest peaks, complete with dozens of glacial basin lakes within the close-knit area. But because they are closer to the Pacific, the Trinity Alps receive more precipitation, feed more streams, and support lusher vegetation than their Sierran counterparts. Similar vegetation zones exist 4,000-5,000 feet lower in the Trinity Alps than in the Sierra.

The Trinity Mountains are obviously not limited to Thompson Peak and the rest of the Trinity Alps. The Trinities comprise California's most extensive wilderness area outside of the Sierra. Northeast of the Trinity Alps, the Trinity Mountains have still more cirque lakes and granite outcrops. And west of the Trinity Alps are the wildest, most isolated areas of the Trinities, roadless and uncut. The Devil's Backbone, a narrow ridgeline and trail which follows the New River south of Salmon Mountain (6,957 feet), leads past North Trinity Mountain (6,362 feet) and thrilling views from the Pacific Ocean to the Trinity Alps and beyond.

In the Salmon Mountains northwest of this wilderness, within their tribal fishing grounds at Ishi Pishi Falls on the lower Klamath River, muscular Karok Indians still stab their traditional triangular "lifting nets," framed by narrow wooden poles twenty feet long and more, into the powerful currents between boulders, scooping out King salmon and occasional eels farther downstream. The river canyon near Weitchpec is precipitous—with the highway threaded to the sides of cliffs on scaffolding, high above twisted rock formations that look like driftwood. Frequently dirtslides and rockslides flood into and across steep canyons, leaving green trees lying half-buried, facing downhill.

Nestled near the southeastern end of the Klamath complex, a triad of man-made lakes collects runoff from mountainsides long ago denuded

Castle Crags State Park in the Klamath Ranges. JEFF GNASS

by smelting emissions and heavy lumbering. Here, the branches of manzanita are as red as sunrise, and the dirt is the color of cayenne pepper.

Eight year-round creeks flow into Whiskeytown Lake from a ridge of high peaks to the west, the tallest of which is Shasta Bally (6,209 feet), towering 5,000 feet above the impounded waters. From the 602-foot-high dam of Shasta Lake, California's largest man-made lake, Mt. Shasta is visible to the north, and limestone caves in the mountains overlooking the lake contain stone draperies and fluted columns sixty feet high.

The third of these lakes, Clair Engle, is the starting point from which the water of the Trinity River, draining 443,000 acres, makes a remarkable journey—traveling through a 10.8-mile tunnel drilled beneath the Trinity Mountains and into Whiskeytown Lake, then down Clear Creek, and

finally swelling the Sacramento River.

Yet, for all their timber and mineral resources, their massive water diversion projects, and their attractions for anglers, hikers, and spelunkers, the Klamath Ranges are probably best known for a creature which may not exist—Bigfoot, Sasquatch, the legendary half-man/half-ape. Despite Indian myths, reported sightings, and a purported film sequence of the huge, hairy creature, there remains no proof that Bigfoot inhabits the Klamath Ranges. Still, small towns here celebrate in honor of the animal every year, curio shops sell plaster casts of Bigfoot tracks, and many residents ignore outsiders who scoff at the notion of a primitive species of man lurking in northern California.

Meanwhile, trees fall in the wild, dark heart of the Klamath Ranges and no human being for miles is there to hear.

The Cascade Range:
High and hot-tempered

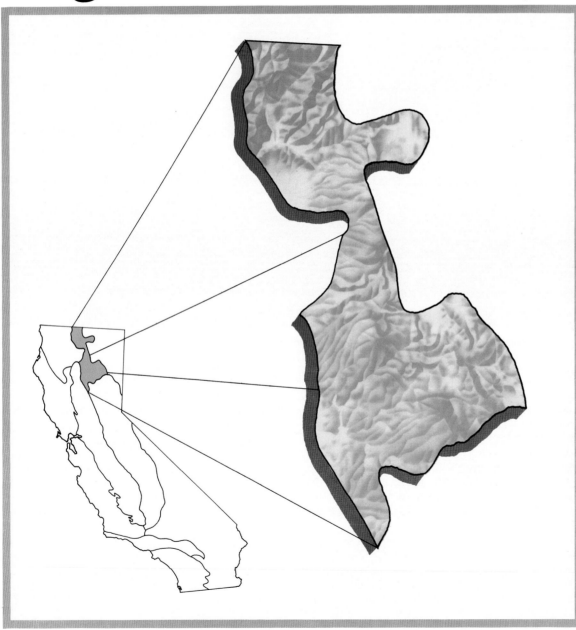

California's Cascade mountains are volcanoes. That is how they are explained, how they are remembered, and how they are treated.

Cascade peaks in California are only the southern stragglers of an angry volcanic mountain range that marches all the way into Canada. One of the newest landforms in the world, the Cascades are fed by the rising gases and melted rock of the Pacific plate subducting deep beneath the North American plate. In California, they begin at Lake Almanor on the Feather River and extend north to the Oregon border. They are bounded on the east by the Modoc Plateau and scattered Basin Ranges, and on the west by Interstate 5 and the Trinity, Scott, and Scott Bar mountains of the Klamath Ranges.

Most geologists believe that the Sierra and Klamath ranges, split apart by massive faulting, were subsequently buried by enormous eruptions of Cascade volcanoes, covering all traces of that faulting and all links between the two ranges. It's evident today, however, that the vast blankets of lava and ash, once thousands of feet thick, prohibit virtually all agriculture and most ranching. The Cascades are a quiet, sparsely populated range covered by young, unimpressive stands of pine and fir. Only after heavy snows do these mountains seem populated—in recently logged clearings where hundreds of black stumps wear ballooning chef's hats of snow, each tilted in precisely the same direction by the wind.

In the 106,000-acre Lassen Volcanic National

Blue flag iris (right) near Grass Lake seems to bask in a warmer climate than the majestic hulk of Mt. Shasta in the background. LARRY ULRICH

Brilliant balsamroot and stately conifers frame this view of Brokeoff Mountain (far right) in Lassen Volcanic National Park. Many geologists believe Brokeoff was originally the lower slope of a giant volcano, Mt. Tehama, which emptied itself during an eruption and collapsed. JEFF GNASS

From high on Cinder Cone in Lassen Volcanic National Park, a mosaic of painted volcanic dunes (above) billows into the distance. Formed by ash and cinders which exploded from Cinder Cone and landed on still-hot lava, the Painted Dunes were colored in places by rising steam which oxidized minerals to hues of red and yellow. JEFF GNASS

As this Lassen Peak-bound climber in snowshoes attests, Lassen Volcanic National Park becomes a winter wonderland for thousands of recreationists when deep snows bury miles and miles of volcanic debris. JEFF GNASS

Park, some dry volcanic rocks are pocked with tiny bubbles; others reflect the sun as if they were glazed. When wet, though, most of this volcanic debris looks like red clay, firm but not brittle. Trees killed by thermal explosions still litter the ground like bodies on a battlefield.

When it first became a national monument in 1906, Lassen Peak (10,457 feet) was considered the best example of an extinct volcano in the United States and the largest plug dome volcano on earth. John Muir noted the mountain chiefly for its south-slope mountain hemlocks, which he considered the finest examples of that species he had ever seen.

May 30, 1914 brought a shock, however—both literally and figuratively. On that memorable Memorial Day, Lassen Peak spewed a towering plume of steam thousands of feet into the air. Within the next three years it erupted 150 times, blasting debris as high as five miles, raining inches of volcanic ash on cities as far away as Reno, Nevada, flushing a river of lava a thousand feet down its slopes, and creating one mud flow eighteen miles long and a quarter-mile wide which buoyed twenty-ton boulders for miles.

The largest explosion blasted away the northeast side of the mountain and rushed on, destroying all vegetation in its path. The peak still provides chilling views of the devastation; of other flat, faulted brown lava flows receding like stairs into the distance; and of Lake Almanor, its fifty-two square miles of azure water curiously serene among evergreen forests.

As unbelievable as it seems, the massive mountain which is now Lassen Peak was once simply an interior dome much like those rising in the crater of Washington's Mt. St. Helens today. Broke-off Mountain (9,235 feet), Mt. Diller (9,087 feet), Mt. Conard (8,204 feet), Pilot Pinnacle (7,175 feet)—all were originally the slopes of an immense, ancient volcano named Mt. Tehama, which collapsed around Lassen Peak ten thousand years ago.

Just northeast of Lassen Peak, astonishingly

symmetrical Cinder Cone is a textbook example of a volcanic cinder cone. Created by sand-sized volcanic grains, the 700-foot-high cone slopes upward on all sides at an angle of almost exactly thirty degrees, about the same incline as a steep sand dune has. Immigrants along the nearby William Noble trail reported seeing Cinder Cone erupt in 1851.

Northwest of Lassen Peak, Chaos Crags (8,503 feet) have created a catastrophe waiting for a signal. The group of three plug dome volcanoes erupted as recently as three hundred years ago, creating Chaos Jumbles, a 150-million-cubic-yard mass of volcanic debris perched precariously above Manzanita Lake. In 1975, park officials closed all overnight facilities in the lake area, fearing that another eruption—or even a small earthquake—could cause millions of tons of rocks over steep slopes to break loose and create a monstrous 80-miles-per-hour avalanche riding a cushion of compressed air.

The smell of sulfur seeps from Bumpass Hell, southeast of Lassen Peak. A plank walkway extends out into bubbling pits of gray mud, and layers of fool's gold sparkle beneath deep turquoise water. Fumaroles, hot springs, and steam vents are everywhere. It doesn't take a geologist to know that these are active mountains.

Between Lassen Peak and Mt. Shasta, Burney Falls beautifully and vividly illustrates the nature of volcanic mountains such as the Cascades. Water which has percolated into the lava and runs underground resurfaces as Burney Creek a half-mile above the 129-foot falls—and from the cliff face of the forked waterfall itself. Black swifts, more commonly found as sea birds living in sea cliffs, dart through the curtain of water to and from cavities behind the falls.

The hundred million gallons of water gushing down Burney Falls every day allows the waterfall to slowly eat its way upstream through the basalt rocks of the Cascades, but not by wearing down its bed as most rivers do. Instead, the unvarying

Snow-clad Lassen Peak is reflected in the surface of Manzanita Lake in Lassen Volcanic National Park. Lassen Peak is the southernmost volcano in the Cascade Range and is still considered active. When it staged its most violent eruption, on May 22, 1915, Lassen spewed ash 30,000 feet into the air, left a devastated area of more than one square mile where no tree was left standing, and destroyed trees as far as three miles away. Lassen remained the only volcano in the contiguous 48 states to erupt during this century until Mount St. Helens exploded in 1980, creating a devastated area nearly 16 miles long and 150 square miles in area. PAT O'HARA

An aerial photo of Mt. Shasta (left), still classified as an active volcano, reveals how completely the 14,162-foot-high mountain dominates the landscape and affects cloud formations. This giant of the Cascade Range is mantled by five small glaciers as well as by Shastina, the smaller cone and crater on its west slope. ROBERT BASSE

Evening lends a quiet mood to Mt. Shasta and Shastina. DAVID MUENCH

flow of underground water which feeds the falls is eroding softer sedimentary rock layers *beneath* the lip of the falls. Periodically, the lip of Burney Falls crumbles, and the falls recede a few feet at a time, creating new twenty-foot-deep emerald pools below and leaving behind a trail of crumbled rocks downstream.

North of Burney Falls, the dawn sunlight shafts into deep canyons through mist and shade, as clearly defined as lasers through smoke. Along creeks, the bare limbs of black oaks are velveted like antlers with green moss. The mountains are steeper and more forested here, and motorists look over embankments at the eye-level tops of ponderosa pines a hundred feet tall, their tips as tiny and delicate as living room Christmas trees.

Mt. Shasta (14,162 feet), the dominant landform of northern California, is the second-highest volcano in the entire Cascade Range. (Washington's Mt. Ranier, with an elevation of 14,406 feet, is the tallest.) It is also the largest, rising more than 10,000 feet from a forested base which is 17 miles in diameter, encompassing a volume of about 80 cubic miles and towering 7,000 feet higher than nearby Cascade peaks. Its rock crown splits huge, invisible air currents like they were rivers, capturing and swirling clouds in its backwater. Five Mt. Shasta glaciers, all above the 10,000-foot level, are nourished by the heavy snows which sometimes provide a year-round ski season for two mountainside resorts.

Mt. Shasta is actually a double volcano. A smaller volcano, Shastina, has emerged on its western flank. The French explorer Comte Jean Francois de Dalaup de La Perouse saw a volcano erupting inland as he sailed along the Pacific Coast of California in 1786. Many of today's geologists believe, and dating of lava flows indicates, that it was Mt. Shasta.

At the base of Mt. Shasta, the sleepy main street of McCloud is illuminated at night by gaslights and showered with the honking of invisible geese, thousands upon thousands of them. Tule Lake, sixty miles to the northeast, witnesses the largest concentration of migratory waterfowl on the North American continent. To the northeast of Mt. Shasta, the easternmost peak of California's Cascades, Mt. Hoffman (7,913 feet), cradles Medicine Lake in a huge crater. And north of Mt. Hoffman, Mt. Dome (6,518 feet) and its narrow ridge shadow the cinder buttes of 47,000-acre Lava Beds National Monument, where lava tubes—some more than a mile long—form underground networks and 293 "caves." The tubes formed when rivers of lava cooled on the outside while continuing to flow and empty on the inside.

Here, sixty Modoc Indians and their chief, Captain Jack, held off nearly six hundred soldiers of the U.S. Army for five months. The Modoc Wars, as the Indians' resistance became known, was California's only real war between Indians and whites. Originally living near Mt. Shasta among timber, lakes, and lava beds, the Modocs were hard pressed by Gold Rush settlers and massacred a group of immigrants in 1852, then waged sporadic raids and battles for the next twelve years. Finally placed on a reservation, Captain Jack and his men refused to stay, returning to their ancestral homelands. The U.S. Army arrived, the Modocs fled to the lava beds, and the two sides fought to a standstill in barren terrain the Indians knew so well. Only the shortage of water defeated the Modocs. They surrendered in 1873.

California's small band of Cascade mountains, on the other hand, is still young, still violent, still stubbornly impeding the coming of the white man. And they have considerably more time.

The Sierra Nevada:

A tale of two Sierras

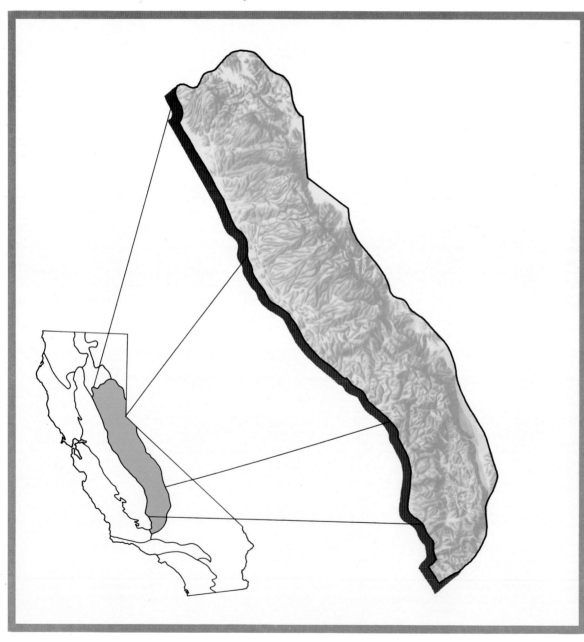

The sky-scraping Sierra Nevada, John Muir's "Range of Light," has no equals. Eight national forests and three enormous national parks do not encompass it. Eleven peaks top 14,000 feet, some five hundred top 12,000 feet, and the range is home to sixty glaciers. Not a single road crosses the Sierra for nearly two hundred miles. It is the largest continuous block of granite on the planet.

Despite its distance from the Pacific Ocean and the cloud-wringing Coast Ranges, the 430-mile-long Sierra is one of the snowiest regions in the world, famous in the north for its wet, heavy "Sierra cement." At Tamarack Lodge (8,000 feet) south of Lake Tahoe, 884 inches of snow fell in the winter of 1906-1907, and yearly averages reach 445 inches. In January 1982, close-by Echo Summit (7,377 feet) claimed the California record for a 24-hour snowfall—67 inches.

The tall southern Sierra creates a soaring, snow-gashed eastern escarpment where fierce granite ridges reach toward the Owens Valley like the forelegs of monstrous animals, spreading into paws and cut into claws—huge alluvial fans formed of sediment washed down by spring melts. The tall Sierra is a range of studded clearings where lodgepole pines have been snapped off nine feet above the ground by avalanches. Walls of baled hay—gold on the sunny south side and still green on the shaded north side—adorn autumn pastures as smooth as manicured fairways. In winter, the interior Sierra is mostly inaccessible, while along peripheral highways like U.S. 395, snowflakes swarm like moths into the headlights of four-wheel-drives carrying anxious skiers.

Beginning in the south near Bakersfield (where the westernmost ridge is often referred to as the Greenhorn Mountains), the Sierra is also the 1.2 million-acre Sequoia National Forest. This is the dry Sierra, often qualifying as desert on some

Luxuriant Pioneer Basin (opposite page) is one of the favorite attractions of the John Muir Wilderness, California's largest. PAT O'HARA

eastern slopes. In contrast with the heavily forested Greenhorn Mountains and the Western Divide, both of which capture the bulk of Pacific moisture, Joshua trees near Walker Pass endure the dry summertime heat, surrendering the arid terrain to chaparral and oak toward Olancha Peak. Sparse pines and firs flee above yucca to the highest elevations, which in the extreme south nowhere exceed 7,000 feet. The Domeland Wilderness, southernmost wilderness in the Sierra, is characteristic of this dry terrain.

Within thirty miles to the north, however, the range becomes more lush. Split by the Kern River, the Golden Trout Wilderness already features such prominent summits as Kern Peak (11,510 feet), Mt. Florence (12,432 feet), and Cirque Peak (12,900 feet), at the southern border of the John Muir Wilderness.

As the Sierra grows, so does its west-slope trees. The most southern of scores of groves of giant sequoia tower from the slopes of ridges above major river canyons. The largest giant sequoia, the General Sherman tree (once named the Karl Marx tree) in 400,000-acre Sequoia National Park, is 272 feet tall, with a volume of more than 50,000 cubic feet. Farther north, in Calaveras Big Trees State Park, visitors can climb to the top of a 24-foot-wide stump, or join arms to circle living trees 35 feet wide.

Giant sequoias occasionally grow to heights of more than three hundred feet. They might well grow even taller, but their tops are frequently blasted by the lightning of frequent inland thunderstorms, a hazard their coastal redwood cousins rarely encounter. Yet even more than coastal redwoods, Sierra redwoods possess

California buckeye climbs above the chasm of lower Kings Canyon. In unusually wet years (the winters of 1969 and 1978, for instance), the Kings River overwhelms manmade levees and diversions downstream, turning often-dry Tulare Lake into the largest freshwater lake in California.
ED COOPER

remarkably delicate features, with tiny leaves and subtle cones.

A similar irony of size is exhibited by the most famous peak in all the Sierra, and perhaps in the United States as well. Mt. Whitney reaches 14,494 feet into the sky above Owens Lake, yet it is not nearly as formidable as many shorter, but steeper, peaks. Only from its own summit does it appear to be the tallest peak. In fact, for years mountain climbers atop Mt. Langley (14,027 feet)—the peak originally named Mt. Whitney—believed they had climbed the Sierra's highest peak until, in 1873, a surveyor proved differently. Two weeks later, three vacationing fishermen from Lone Pine became the first to scale the unnamed mountain, and the name "Mt. Whitney" was transferred to its current location.

Today, an easy ten-mile trail leads to the top and the two-room stone shelter there. Climbers wearing bathing suits, carrying suitcases, and even pushing wheelbarrows have stepped onto Whitney's crest, as have many loaded horses and mules. On one Labor Day, before Whitney climbers were limited to seventy-five daily, a helicopter was necessary to remove the garbage left atop the peak by 1,500 celebrants. A toilet has even been installed on the summit plateau.

Mt. Whitney suffers in appearance because of its company, five other peaks higher than 14,000 feet. To the south, the illustrious fraternity includes Mt. Langley, the southernmost 14,000-footer in the Sierra, its flat crown notched where huge granite boulders have been displaced by frost, and Mt. Muir (14,015 feet). Just north of Mt. Whitney stand Mt. Russell (14,086 feet), Mt. Tyndall (14,018 feet), and Mt. Williamson (14,375

Yosemite National Park's Nevada Falls slides 594 feet over granite which is fractured parallel to the cliff face of Half Dome. Liberty Cap, the high rock dome just beyond Nevada Falls, was buried beneath a thousand feet of ice during the ice age which carved Yosemite Valley. PAT O'HARA

The Sierra Nevada offers incredibly diverse recreational opportunities, guaranteeing adventure for backpackers, mountain climbers, skiers, hunters, prospectors, photographers, history buffs, birdwatchers, canoeists, cyclists, rock collectors, and even sightseeing motorists who never have to leave a paved road.

A solitary angler (left) explores the deep pools and water-smoothed boulders of Bald Rock Canyon on the Middle Fork Feather River. Feather Falls downstream, at 640 feet, is the sixth largest in the United States. JEFF GNASS

A hang glider (above) launches himself into the spectacular sky above Yosemite Valley. Nevada Falls and Vernal Falls below it are visible in the valley, plunging over granite cliffs at right angles to each other. DONALD F. MATTUSCH

feet), the latter the state's second-highest peak.

The headwaters of the Kern River split the range near Mt. Williamson and have created the only major north-south canyon in the Sierra. The Great Western Divide branches southwest from the main Sierra crest. The divide reaches its highest elevation (13,666 feet) at Midway Mountain, while Black Kaweah (13,765 feet), the Sierra's most forbidding peak, rules a spur ridge that is one of the most jagged and remote sections of the range. And one of the most outstanding features of this Kern Plateau region is Monache Meadows, the largest meadow in the Sierra Nevada.

West of Big Pine, the Sierra peaks are clustered into another clique, where the finest alpine climbing in California is found—the North and South Palisades. The remaining five of the range's eleven peaks over 14,000+ feet high keep company here along a nine-mile section of the Sierra crest. Extending from Split Mountain (14,058 feet) above Tenemaha Reservoir in the south, the Palisades include Middle Palisade (14,040 feet); Mt. Sill (14,162 feet), the most massive of the Palisades and generally considered to offer the finest view in all of the Sierra; North Palisade (14,242 feet), the highest of the Palisades and home of California's largest glacier, which covers a square mile; and Thunderbolt Peak (14,000+ feet), its steep, stubborn, monolithic summit in 1931 proving the last of the Sierra's 14,000-footers to be conquered. The latter three peaks form the highest continuous ridge in the entire range. Mt. Agassiz (13,891 feet) is the northernmost peak in the Palisades.

West of the Sierra crest from the Palisades, the headwaters of the Kings River drain 500,000-acre Kings Canyon National Park. Where the South and Middle Forks of the Kings River converge below Junction Ridge, the floor of the fabulous Kings Canyon trough is 8,200 near-vertical feet below, about 2,000 feet deeper than the Grand Canyon.

At the northern end of Kings Canyon National Park, a group of four peaks ring an area known as Evolution Basin, where broad snow fields are often dimpled with deep snow cups formed by uneven thawing. A charter member of John Muir's Sierra Club, Theodore Solomons, named the four peaks after the most famous evolutionists of the day—Mt. Darwin (13,830 feet) for Charles Darwin; Mt. Wallace (13,377 feet) for Alfred Wallace; Mt. Huxley (13,117 feet) for Thomas Huxley; and Mt. Spencer (12,400+ feet) for Herbert Spencer.

North of Sequoia-Kings Canyon and the Evolution Basin, isolated Mt. Humphreys (13,986 feet)—one of the premier mountainclimbing attractions of the High Sierra—presides over the 500,000-acre John Muir Wilderness. For most of a hundred miles, the crest of the High Sierra forms the eastern boundary of California's largest wilderness, which brackets Sequoia-Kings Canyon National Parks as well.

Just outside the northern boundary of the Muir Wilderness, Mammoth Mountain (11,053 feet) on the Sierra crest separates the Mammoth Lakes resorts to the east from Devil's Postpile National Monument on the west. Two gondolas, three surface lifts, and sixteen chairlifts drape the slopes of Mammoth Mountain, making it the largest ski location in the nation. During ski weekends an average of ten thousand skiers daily track the snow of this single mountain.

At Devil's Postpile, great, faceted pillars of basalt, as aligned and polished as the flutes of a massive pipe organ, form a cliff sixty feet high. The incredible formation resulted when deep lava cooled rapidly, shrinking and cracking vertically. A subsequent glacier sheared off the surface of the formation, creating a top as beautifully patterned and polished as any tile floor while depositing a rubble heap of the broken six-sided pillars which now serve as a staircase for climbers.

Across the crest from Mono Lake, the Sierra's sheerest walls, its lushest meadows, its most remarkable monoliths and highest, most breathtaking waterfalls are all associated with a seven-square-mile valley—Yosemite.

This gouged valley is not the deepest in the

California's greatest postman

His name was John A. Thompson, but he is known as "Snow-shoe." His ten-foot-long, six-inch-wide, twenty-five pound oak skis are on display at Plumas-Eureka State Park. The feats of this Norwegian immigrant are legendary.

Between 1856 and 1876, "Snow-shoe" Thompson carried the mail across the Sierra during the winter, between Placerville and Genoa, Nevada. He always traveled alone, eating jerky and biscuits, and never carried a blanket or even a heavy coat. With loads of eighty pounds on his back, he could complete the 110-mile journey east over 7,735-foot Luther Pass in three days. The return trip took him only two. He never got lost or hurt, despite violent blizzards. And he was never paid.

Other Norwegians, gold miners, challenged Thompson to a race once. Wagers were made, onlookers gathered, and Thompson—unaware of the "dope" applied to the bottoms of his opponents' skis—was humiliated. He responded with a challenge of his own, daring anyone to follow him for one day, "from top to bottom of the highest and steepest mountain we can find" and "over a precipice fifteen feet high, without use of a pole," without breaking a neck. No one dared.

"Snow-shoe" died in the spring of 1876. His simple tombstone in Genoa, Nevada, is engraved with two remarkably delicate skis.

Sierra, nor is it the longest. But a titanic, slow battle between glaciers and granite left the largest unfractured piece of granite on the face of the earth here—majestic El Capitan, 3,464 feet from top to bottom, exeeding Gibraltar in mass, and dwarfing the sky. The highest waterfall in the United States is here, too—Yosemite Falls, tumbling and free-falling in a three-tiered drop of 2,425 feet.

Yosemite National Park, all 1,200 square miles of it, was in large measure the gift of naturalist John Muir to humankind. It was first explored in 1851 by volunteer soldiers in pursuit of marauding Indians. One young man recorded his reaction: "As I looked, a peculiar exalted sensation seemed to fill my whole being, and I found my eyes in tears with emotion."

Yet soon afterwards, the white granite walls of Yosemite—formerly colored only by the likes of 620-foot Bridalveil Falls, which has soaked the rock soot-black with algae—were painted with commercial advertising. An 1864 act of Congress, the first federal action setting aside wildlands, gave Yosemite protection as a state park. Muir, however, was not satisfied, and his efforts and influence were instrumental in congressional approval of an expansion of the park and its transfer back to the federal government as a *national* park.

Today, three million tourists visit Yosemite every year, vying for two thousand campsites and employing five hundred park employees and two thousand concessionaires. A typical year involves two hundred search and rescue operations and more than twenty fatalities. On one Fourth of July weekend, sixteen mounted park rangers and twenty-one riot-helmeted reinforcements charged a meadow full of young people partying and beating bongos, arresting nearly two hundred. And as recently as 1967, Yosemite staged its own regular fireworks show, with burning embers pushed from atop Glacier Point at night to the applause of crowds below.

Undoubtedly the most popular outcrop above Yosemite, Glacier Point overlooks the valley in both directions. Across the tiny Merced River below, Half Dome—the largest single feature of Yosemite—rises nearly a mile above the floor of Tenaya Canyon. Trails of white mist and gossamer-thin rainbows accompany Vernal Falls on its 317-foot plunge, while 594-foot Nevada Falls roars like an eternal gale.

Unlike the valley floor, crowded with cars, tourists, camera tripods, and skiers (who use the valley as a parking lot, then ride buses to Badger Pass), Yosemite's Cathedral Peak backcountry is a more peaceful expanse of splendid scenery. Here, undrowned by the noise of horns and hordes, visitors can hear the low, faraway rumble of the park's occasional massive landslides, and feel the faint vibrations in the pits of their stomachs, like adrenalin. Five High Sierra camps not accessible by road are maintained for hikers and saddle riders, with dormitory tents clustered around large dining tents where family-style meals are served.

The Tuolumne River, fed by glaciers on Mt. Lyell (13,114 feet)—highest peak in both the Cathedral Range and Yosemite National Park—meanders through the lush open of Tuolumne Meadows before carving its own wider and less accessible canyon. In 1882, the canyon became a focal point of one of the first great environmentalist battles—and losses—when O'Shaughnessy Dam was proposed as part of the Hetch Hetchy reservoir-and-aqueduct system to carry water to the San Francisco Bay Area. Approval of the dam in 1913

Snow comes to life

When John Muir first shouted "A living glacier!" upon realizing how Yosemite Valley had been shaped, he had no idea how dynamic these rivers of ice really are.

Intricate snowflakes, weighing ten times less than water, pack against each other and become tiny balls of ice which meld themselves together even if temperatures dip below freezing. They become powder snow, twice as heavy and twice as strong as snowflakes. As they pack tighter, they increase in weight and strength.

By the time snowflakes become glacial ice, perhaps years after falling, they increase in weight ninefold and in strength five hundred fold. They become dense crystals of rock-hard ice as long as ten inches.

The lives of glaciers, especially younger and smaller ones, are recorded in layers of ice just as accurately as the lives of trees are recorded in their rings or the lives of sedimentary rock formations are recorded in their strata. Layers of glacial ice vary in air and dirt content, reflecting weather conditions. Even more amazing, pollen content may make it possible to trace layers to particular seasons.

Not only do glaciers move up and down mountains and through valleys—they also move within themselves. The center of a glacier moves faster than its outer edges, because of the effects of drag. Moreover, when a glacier becomes 100-150 feet thick, its molecules begin to shift, much like the roiling billows in a cloud, so that a glacier moving over rocks may actually act as a vacuum cleaner, drawing objects inside. Like the folding and pulverizing of rock strata, these movements within the ice can destroy records of the glacier's formation.

Finally, just as the immense compression of rocks deep within the earth heats them enough to melt, the compression inside a glacier often causes it to melt from the inside. Streams of water flow deep within some glaciers, almost like circulating blood, confined to ice tubes they have made themselves. A living glacier!

A long-abandoned miner's shack (far left) ages gracefully beside Ward Creek in the northern Sierra Nevada. At the height of the California gold rush, rumors flew of a lake where Indians had knocked out square blocks of gold for chairs and couches, of streams where gold could be scraped from the banks by the pound, and of prospectors who discarded any chunks of gold which had quartz sticking to them.
CARR CLIFTON

A modern-day prospector (top), his hand insulated from the icy water by a rubber glove, empties dirt and rock into a sluice, where tiny flecks of gold among the riffles will settle to the bottom.
CARR CLIFTON

Mining is not, however, the only major industry depending on California's mountains. Both yesterday and today, logging has, without doubt, had a major influence on California's economy, thanks to the incredibly rich forest resources blanketing most mountain ranges. Here a logger uses his chainsaw (bottom) to thin a section of Plumas National Forest in the northern Sierra.
CARR CLIFTON

drowned some of the canyon's wildest sections.

Still more primitive areas surround the park itself. To the southeast, the John Muir Trail leads into the Ansel Adams (formerly the Minarets) Wilderness at Donohue Pass, below Mt. Ritter (13,157 feet), a striking Sierra landmark visible from peaks eighty miles downrange. A group of shattered Sierra peaks known as the Ritter Range, their deadly ledges strewn with rock debris, dominates the Sierra to the south. And Mt. Dana (13,053 feet), marking the northern tip of the wilderness, guards the Tioga Pass entrance to Yosemite.

Along the northeast border of Yosemite National Park, the narrow Hoover Wilderness borders the Sierra crest for nearly twenty-five miles. Nowhere

is the wilderness—much of it above timberline—more than five miles wide, and at one point it is barely a mile wide. Yet it traces the Sawtooth Ridge, where clean white granite peaks and frequent if small glaciers signal the beginning of the High Sierra. Matterhorn Peak (12,264 feet), which has five remnant glaciers of its own, is higher than any Sierra peak farther north.

Immediately north of Yosemite National Park, the 106,000-acre Emigrant Wilderness, blanketed by snow from October to June, rises through rocky domes and deep granite canyons to Leavitt Peak (11,570 feet) near Sonora Pass. The Emigrant Basin, where the wilderness is centered, contains more than a hundred high trout lakes, the largest concentration of alpine lakes in the Sierra. Hiking

trails here follow paths used by Gold Rush-era emigrants, and wagon ruts are still visible in places.

Between Sonora Pass and Lake Tahoe, the Sierra is a range rich with volcanic deposits. While the granite block of the Sierra was still young and rising, massive volcanic eruptions from the east buried most of the exposed granite. Glaciers which followed carried away much of this volcanic debris from the High Sierra to the south, but here deep volcanic deposits still remain.

The contrast between vegetation on adjacent volcanic and granitic slopes is often striking. Only sparse grasses and scattered wildflowers are able to survive in the thin soils underlain by granite. But in deeper, volcanic-enriched soils, fairly lush grass and profuse displays of wildflowers thrive. Not surprisingly, hikers in this portion of the Sierra are almost as likely to encounter cattle or sheep as they are to see wildlife, since thousands of grazing livestock roam these green public lands leased to ranchers.

Standing like a volcanic island among the sea of granite, the Dardenelles rise more than a thousand feet above the surrounding heavily forested landscape in the Carson-Iceberg Wilderness, part of 1.1 million-acre Stanislaus National Forest. And timber thrives in these volcanic soils. In 586,000-acre Eldorado National Forest just north of the Dardenelles, for example, more than 135 million board feet of lumber—enough to build 14,000 average-sized houses—is sold every year.

Lake Tahoe, nestled 6,228 feet high in the Sierra and the second-highest lake of its size in the world, is a natural lake more than fifteen hundred feet deep in places. Its depth accounts for both its crystalline waters and the fact that it never freezes

Sevehan Cliff soars above the Sierra's Convict Lake, formed in the end of a glacial trough and dammed by moraines. MICHAEL S. SAMPLE

over. Both qualities have made it a mountain resort of world renown, surrounded now by nineteen ski areas including Squaw Valley, site of the 1960 Winter Olympics.

The most dazzling views come from a road circling high above the south end of Lake Tahoe, where the lake's only island, Fannette, is surrounded by Emerald Bay. Here too, although hidden behind lordly sugar pines splattered with snow, is a thirty-eight room mansion, "Vikingsholm," patterned after a ninth-century Norse fortress and perfectly appropriate among Tahoe's vertical cliffs and inlets to match any fjords.

In the 1840s, the explorer John Fremont first named the lake Bonpland, after a French botanist. The lake was renamed in 1852 to honor California's Governor Bigler. But during the Civil War, Bigler's Southern sympathies angered a mapmaker who arbitrarily renamed the lake Tahoe, the Washoe Indian word for "big water." It has remained Lake Tahoe ever since.

Perhaps not the same Lake Tahoe first viewed by Fremont, however. Casinos, limos, and wedding chapels flash on its Nevada shores. On still days, brown woodsmoke and smog settle into the Tahoe basin. And deep beneath its crystal surface, Lake Tahoe is steadily accumulating the sewage of lakeside developments.

Immediately southwest of Lake Tahoe, the 64,000-acre Desolation Wilderness lives up to its name—vast areas are nearly devoid of trees, planted instead with huge boulders among the glacier-polished slopes. Near Echo Summit, a major pass to Lake Tahoe, Pyramid Peak (9,983 feet) rises highest from the wilderness, above more than seventy pristine lakes.

When John Muir called the Sierra Nevada the "Range of Light," he had in mind the Sierra of awesome granite peaks, living glaciers, and deep, misty valleys—"the sunbursts of mornings among the icy peaks, the noonday radiance on the trees and rocks and snow, the flush of the alpen glow, and a thousand dashing waterfalls with their marvellous abundance of irised spray...."

But there is another Sierra range. Topographic maps and aerial photographs are unable to distinguish this "other" Sierra from Muir's beloved peaks to the east, and geologists are smugly convinced that there is only one Sierra Nevada. But most Californians know better.

Just as the high Sierra passes were discovered by white explorers, although Indians had used them for centuries, the "other" Sierra was not really discovered until 1848, when James Marshall found gold at Sutter's Mill, on the American River near the present-day town of Coloma. The "Range of Riches" parallels the Sierra crest along its entire length. It is a lower Sierra, stunning not because of its peaks but because of its gravels. The important elevations are still measured in thousands of feet, but here they record not the heights of peaks but the depths of mineshafts.

The most poetic lights emanating from these Sierra mountains came from lustrous gold and the eyes and lanterns of miners. Even today, lifelong prospectors, wearing rubber gloves as they pan the icy streams for tiny nuggets worth a dollar, still

This cinder cone in the dry shadow of the Sierra Nevada near Big Pine was formed by hot volcanic sand spewing from the earth. Originally black, it turned red as iron in the lava granules rusted. Such miniature volcanoes form elsewhere, too, but do not last long in wet climates where they erode quickly. MICHAEL WEEKS

move from canyon to canyon and campfire to campfire, living on pensions and in no hurry. Today, not even Muir's Range of Light is more colorful.

Traveling east from the smooth, irrigated Central Valley, the smaller Sierra resembles a rising sea. Gentle swells of earth ripple with pastures. Then the ground pitches higher, its waves crested with oaks and boulders. Telephone poles cross great, treeless ridges like harpoons. Finally, the stormy peaks of the "other" Sierra crest loom to the east, foaming white with snow.

But despite the gradual rise of the Range of Riches—mild compared to the mighty tidal wave of the High Sierra's eastern face—the lower western slopes of the Sierra Nevada in many ways are just as rugged as the highest peaks. Veins of red dirt seep like huge springs from the steep walls of canyons, cut by hundreds of rivers and streams flowing west from the snows and glaciers above. Countless more gulches run red with mud after every downpour.

North-south travel over such terrain is extremely slow and tortuous, and today many travelers find it charming as well. But when muleskinners and jerkline teams carried heavy freight to the mines, the "Mule Ballet" was performed here, along steep, primitive roads and hairpin curves. Lead mules would have plunged into canyons, carrying wagons and supplies with them, except that mules farther back were trained to jump over their chains and pull in the opposite direction. And even in the northern Range of Riches, where elevations generally do not exceed 6,000 feet, construction of the Feather River Highway (California 70) required nine bridges and three tunnels through outcroppings of solid granite.

As surely as geologic cataclysms millions of years ago endowed these Sierra foothills with precious metals, the social cataclysm of the Gold Rush—the greatest human migration of all time—endowed them with precious history, exposed by chance here and there and more often mined for all it is worth. Placerville citizens want to revive the town's previous name, Hangtown. The walking tour of Plymouth features Caucasian Hall (described by contemporaries as "a credit to the order"). Above Angels Camp, the original chimney and fireplace of Mark Twain's cabin look down from grassy Jackass Hill, a stopover for packers carrying supplies to miners and named for the hundreds of mules which spent the night there, serenading the countryside. Dozens of other towns in these Sierra foothills use cables like corsets to steady sagging stone facades, and they all seem to have historical markers and driveways lined with gold-painted boulders.

Differences of opinion

Josiah Whitney, one of the most important historical figures in California mountains, is more famous for being wrong than for being right.

Whitney, a graduate of Yale, was head of the California State Geological Survey, which first undertook the Herculean job of mapping the mountains of California.

He left his name on California's highest peak. He also had a profound impact on Yosemite Valley. He published the first guidebooks to Yosemite, bringing it national attention, and was the first to use the term "national park."

Whitney strongly disagreed with John Muir on the subject of Yosemite Valley. Muir, of course, was the Scotsman who came to California from Wisconsin, spent a decade making a fortune growing fruit, and then founded the Sierra Club and became the father of the conservation movement. His early writings helped guarantee protection for the newly famous valley.

Disagreeing with Whitney, who for years had proclaimed that Yosemite Valley was the result of faulting, Muir presumptuously published his own opinions (later proved correct) that the incomparable walls and formations of Yosemite had been carved by glaciers.

In a public announcement, Whitney responded vehemently, calling Muir "a mere sheepherder, an ignoramus"—adding, "a more absurd theory was never advanced....This theory, based on entire ignorance of the whole subject, may be dropped without wasting any more time upon it."

Whitney's most embarrassing blunder, however, involved the "Calaveras Skull,"allegedly discovered in a mineshaft near Cherokee Flat. Whitney claimed in treatises and at scientific conventions that the prehistoric skull proved his long-held opinion that man inhabited Calaveras County millions of years earlier than anyone else thought.

Unfortunately for Whitney, if not for science, it turned out that the skull had been stolen from a doctor's office by local practical jokers and stuffed into the gravel of the mine.

Rock Creek begins its Sierran journey from Little Lakes Basin to the Owens Valley, thousands of feet below. MARGARET MALM/NATURE PIX

Towns erupted and eroded as the mountains surrounding them had, if somewhat more quickly. Graniteville, for instance, with a population now measured in the dozens even in the busy summer months, was once a bustling town of hydraulic miners and merchants near Nevada City. It boasted one of the world's first telephone lines, installed just two years after Alexander Graham Bell unveiled his invention in Boston. But Graniteville is far more isolated now than it was then—without telephones, or electricity, or even snowplows to clear the roads in winter.

Across the Yuba River from Graniteville, the mining camps of Forest and Alleghany, separated by miles of Sierra foothills, were once connected by mining tunnels. Among the rolling ridges west of Yosemite, Mariposa still uses the two-story courthouse built there in 1854, and its tower clock—built in an era when watches were scarce, expensive, and taxed—has been ringing hours to the slopes since 1866. In Tuttletown, the remains of Swerer's Store have outlasted the remains of Bret Harte, who clerked there, and Twain, who shopped there. Carson Hill, just across the Stanislaus River, is still ventilated to depths of 5,000 feet by fifteen miles of tunnels, where the richest of all Mother Lode strikes produced a single nugget that weighed 195 pounds.

Colors in the Range of Riches are not always so gay or quaint. At Jackson, north of the Mokelumne River, the rusted gallows frames of the Kennedy and Argonaut gold mines still creak below the outcropped brow of Jackson Butte. The 5,570-foot-deep Argonaut mine was the site of the worst gold mining tragedy in California history. Forty-seven miners died two miles beneath the earth, in a mine fire which belched deadly gases.

The Malakoff mine near Nevada City was the largest hydraulic gold mine in the world—a scar 7,000 feet long, 3,000 feet wide, and nearly 600 feet deep in places, surrounded by open meadows, deep canyons, and oak-wreathed slopes. One of the wonders of technology, hydraulic mining made it economical to mine gravel containing less than a nickel's worth of gold per cubic yard. Miners directed high pressure water hoses—the jets of spray from the nozzles could kill a man at two hundred feet—at ridges and pits to blast loose dirt and gravel. Thousands of such operations scarred mountains throughout California, leaving behind vast rubbish piles of boulders and murky, silted rivers. An 1884 California court decision ended hydraulic mining abruptly, however, by prohibiting the dumping of tailings into California rivers—a practice which had angered downstream farmers.

The northernmost Sierra is drained by the three branches of the Feather River, which has the greatest water flow out of the entire range. Named by a Spanish explorer who found the water swirling with feathers of migrating band-tailed pigeons, the river forms a three-fingered lake behind the highest dam in the United States and the highest earth-fill dam in the world—the 770-foot Oroville Dam.

East of Lake Oroville, the towering, jagged Sierra Buttes (8,587 feet) are ringed by lake basins and visible for miles around. No Sierra mountain to the north of these dramatic peaks is higher.

Yet the Range of Riches is hardly played out. The Middle Fork of the Feather River, protected under the Wild and Scenic Rivers Act, flows through punishing Bald Rock Canyon, impenetrable except by expert floaters. Not even a foot trail descends there. And 640-foot Feather Falls on a nearby tributary is the sixth-highest falls in the continental United States.

If the Sierra here plays out at all, it is not to the north, where even geologists cannot agree where the Sierra Nevada ends and the Cascade Range begins. It is rather to the west, where the broad, flat plain of the Sacramento Valley washes against the range. Rising from that plain, northwest of Yuba City, are the Sutter Buttes, dwarfing grassland windmills into tiny steel flowers with missing petals.

The sudden, unusual Sutter Buttes are not really

The exfoliating granite surfaces of North Dome and Basket Dome, seen here from Washburn Point, rise above the spectacular Yosemite Valley. MARGARET MALM/NATURE PIX

part of the Sierra Nevada. In fact, they are not a part of *any* other mountain range. They are a tiny volcanic range unto themselves, arguably the smallest identifiable mountain range in the world. Rising to an elevation of only 2,132 feet, the only snow they usually see is in the backs of skiers' pickups returning from Lake Tahoe. Yet they are far more visible than any more celebrated, more photographed, more profitable Sierra peak—of either Sierra range.

What a relief

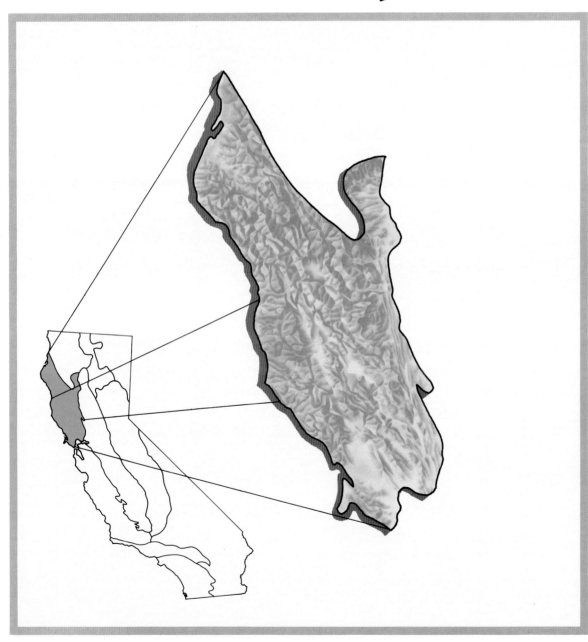

A mountain is more than mere elevation, and California's North Coast Ranges prove that more vividly than any others in the state. Stretching south from the Klamath River, South Fork Mountains, and along the Central Valley all the way to San Francisco Bay, the peaks of the North Coast Ranges make up in relief—the difference between the base and peak of a mountain—what they lack in sheer height. The tallest Sierra peaks, for instance, exceed 13,000 feet in elevation but many begin at the edge of the Owens Valley almost 7,000 feet above sea level. Moreover, many of the Sierra peaks do not become identifiable—distinguishable from surrounding peaks—until thousands of feet higher.

In comparison, the highest of the North Coast Ranges, the South Yolla Bolla Mountains, exceeds 8,000 feet elevation above the Sacramento Valley, more than 7,000 feet below. ''Smaller'' 4,000-to-6,000-foot-high North Coast Ranges peaks, rising from at or near sea level, may also be more prominent in terms of relief than many more-celebrated Sierra peaks. The result is an entire region of California where the eye, not the altimeter, is the most reliable measure of mountains.

With some exceptions, the North Coast Ranges are not a major focus of outdoor recreation such as backpacking and mountain climbing, although hunting and fishing are popular. Instead, these mountains for the most part are devoted to logging (unlike the great forests of the Sierra and around Lake Tahoe, where tourism is a more important resource than timber), to cattle and sheep ranching, and to isolated pockets of agriculture in the south.

In the northern regions of the North Coast Ranges, logging trucks curl like insects up the mountainsides, trunks protruding from their segmented bodies like stingers. Here, along the westernmost slopes and a few miles inland, grow the coastal redwoods, tallest trees on earth. Pacific rains drench these slopes with 40-80 inches of rain annually, and fog condensing on leaves and dropping to the ground can add another seventeen inches of precipitation a year. Beneath the green canopies, daylight has a soft, bluish glow and voices echo until they are replaced by whispers. The drone of a light plane becomes the buzz of an insignificant fly.

Furrows in the bark of mature coastal redwoods are wider and deeper than any arm, twisted at the base as if the trees were no more than weeds to be pulled. Adding to such bizarre illusions of size are clusters of magnificent trunks sharing the same roots, again like common weeds. Yet what an eruption of energy it must have taken, even if spent over thousands of years, to thrust these trees to such heights.

In the backyards of mobile homes tucked into these lush mountains, redwood stumps twelve feet across hold piles of scrap lumber or send up new, bright green sprouts in the shadows of satellite dishes. Twisting, one-lane dirt roads divide vertical walls of towering redwoods on one side from graveyard slopes of charred stumps on the other, where lumber companies will reseed with faster-growing Douglas firs. Helicopters will also spray hundreds of thousands of acres like these with herbicides periodically, killing competing brush and deciduous trees. In fact, the volumes of chemicals applied to these mountains and in the Klamath Ranges to the north and east rivals in tonnage the amounts of agricultural insecticides sprayed on the Central Valley.

San Francisco was originally built from these trees, and the region's worst flood in recorded history—the massive weeks-long flood of 1964—occurred in the wake of large-scale logging activities here and farther inland, activities such

Arum lilies, their leaves as beautiful as their blossoms, thrive on the Sonoma Coast north of San Francisco. RENE PAULI

as clear-cutting which increased the erosion of some slopes 1,700 percent.

The rainforest vegetation near the north coast evaporates, however, beyond the first sizeable inland ridges, replaced by Douglas fir, tanoak, madrone, and oak. These drier hollows may be no more than a mile or two from lush pockets of ferns and redwoods, but they are farther inland where fog is less frequent.

Southeast of Eureka, between the valleys of the Van Duzen and Mad rivers, the Coast Ranges are an eerie, primitive world of grassy berms among oaks furred with fluorescent lime-green lichens. In crevices and valleys, thick white fogs are the ghosts of glaciers which never appeared here. In these mists, the sun can cross the sky as weak as headlights on the highway, and the moon becomes a diffused light above murky water.

If a person wanted to flee southern California, few places are as remote as these mountains of northern California, where horses scramble like mountain goats in their steep corrals and brace themselves to drink from amputated pickup beds. The unpaved road to Kneeland is every bit as curved as San Francisco's Lombard Street, but here there are sheer cliffs rather than curbs and dripping Spanish moss rather than bright flowers. Only an occasional tie-dyed flag is proof that this is still, indeed, the same California.

Farther south, the King Range, California's "Lost Coast," is so rugged that it forces California 1 farther from the coast than at any other point between San Diego and Oregon. This area is the most sparsely populated section of the northern California coast. Kings Peak (4,087 feet) dominates this range, rising from the ocean in less than three miles, the steepest incline from peak to ocean along the entire West Coast. Below, the ocean foam at Shelter Cove is as white as snow, and patches of seaweed add glossy patterns to the contour lines of incoming waves.

Perhaps nothing illustrates more clearly the jumbled, erosive nature of California's North Coast Ranges than the trails leading to Kings Peak. Downslope oaks and madrones might as well have been hit by shotgun blasts, scarred as they are by the loose boulders that crash repeatedly from above. Undergrowth is tunneled by rockslide trails more than by animal trails. Push a rock out of the road and it disappears within feet, but the resulting landslide of loose shale will last for several minutes, receding with the sound of a heavy downpour on pavement, punctuated by the crack of branches and thuds of larger collisions. Fortunately, the eastern slopes of the King Range are more gentle, a characteristic of many North Coast Ranges.

Local legends say a Spanish galleon was wrecked off Cape Mendocino once, and that Indians hid treasures washed ashore in a Kings Peak cave which was later closed by an earthquake. Local history recites another legend of treasure—the tiny town of Petrolia, hidden at the north end of the range, was the site of the first oil well in California.

Inland from the King Range, agriculture is more common than farther north. Backyard vineyards increase in number and size to the east. But it is still steep—in places, the top of one fencepost is level with the bottom of the next.

Well east of the King Range in the Yolla Bolly-Middle Eel Wilderness, the North Coast Ranges give rise to the headwaters of the Eel River. This is one of the least-visited wilderness areas in California, offering spectacular hiking through stands of pine with minimal understory and a large black bear population. South Yolla Bolly Mountain (8,092 feet) towers above the southern portion of the wilderness.

The peaks of Black Butte (7,448 feet), Snow

Grass on the other side of the hill

The mountains of California's North Coast and Klamath ranges can be treacherous—not only because of landslides, floods, rattlesnakes, and black bears, but also because of marijuana fields. Officials estimate that half of California's $2 billion annual marijuana harvest occurs in these remote mountains.

Hikers stumbling onto fields of marijuana on public land have been shot at and threatened. They have encountered electrical alarm systems, guard dogs, booby-trapped shotguns, eye-level fish hooks, and even sharpened stakes at the bottoms of concealed pits. One field was guarded by a leopard, three tigers, and a pack of Doberman pinschers.

Increased marijuana cultivation in California's mountains, where plots of eight thousand plants twenty feet tall have been discovered, is the result of several factors. Since they are rent-free and remote, public lands have always been attractive to some growers. But tough new laws allowing the property of convicted pot growers to be confiscated have spurred hundreds of small-time growers to head for the mountains as well. Economic slumps, especially hard on lumbermen and farmers, make the lucrative, but risky, pot market tempting, and local hardware and fertilizer stores benefit, too. Marijuana is now the state's third-largest cash crop, trailing only grapes and cotton.

Whatever the reasons, growers are becoming more sophisticated. One (unsuccessfully) decorated marijuana plants with red Christmas-tree balls to look like tomato plants from the air. Another used water beds on a mountainside to provide drip irrigation. Whole fields are now grown underground in irrigated pits covered with fiberglass and even green grass to make them invisible to infrared photographs taken from surveillance aircraft.

Mountain (7,056 feet) and Mt. Sanhedrin (6,175 feet) in Mendocino National Forest signal a steady drop in the elevations of major North Coast Range peaks, a trend which continues all the way to San Francisco Bay. As the increasingly dry slopes of North Coast Ranges sink toward the Russian River from both east and west, oak and California bay laurels predominate. Ring-necked pheasant and California quail are here. Tiny blacktail deer often slink out of sight, their tails between their legs; but the fallow deer—imported by Randolph Hearst, who owned a ranch near Willits, are even more shy, rarely seen except at a distance. The does are frequently mistaken for goats, but bucks of the species have distinctive flat palmate racks, much like caribou.

Beyond the crest of the Mayacamas, much of the terrain is wrinkled and bulbous and bare. Horses graze among barn-sized boulders. Towering on either side above Clear Lake, the largest natural lake entirely in California, are the area's highest peaks, Pine Mountain (4,420 feet) and Pinnacle Peak (4,618 feet) to the northeast and Mt. Konocti (4,299 feet) to the southwest. Between them, outboard boats tow water skiers around and around Bloody Island, where more than a hundred Pomo Indians—men, women, and children—were herded and massacred by soldiers in 1849.

South of Clear Lake, the smoldering Mayacamas mountainsides near Cobb Mountain (4,722 feet) spew tiny tornadoes of steam. Newcomers usually remark at the smell of rotten eggs, sulfur fumes which local residents have learned to ignore. The Geysers, Pacific Gas and Electric's geothermal facilities here, were the nation's first geothermal

A mountain stream cascades over and around moss-coated rocks in the 2.8-million-acre Trinity National Forest in the North Coast Ranges. More than half of the annual precipitation in the North Coast Ranges occurs from December to February, so by late summer many small streams such as this are dry. JEFF GNASS

energy project and contain the world's largest geothermal generating unit. The Geysers produces as much electricity as a good-sized nuclear plant.

None of the natural steam vents here are tapped; they would be too corroding. Instead, more than three hundred wells have been drilled, some two miles deep, to tap "clean" steam which still must be cleansed of tiny rock particles. The steam travels through oilfield-type valves at 2.7 million pounds of pressure an hour and pings through insulated pipes, mounted on the rugged slopes like handrails, on its way to generating units where it turns humming turbines to produce electricity. The spent steam is then condensed in giant bushelbasket cooling towers, some of it to be injected back into the earth.

Despite the production of relatively clean energy, The Geysers are controversial here. Virtually all geothermal development has occurred in Sonoma County. Just across the crest of the Mayacamas, in Lake County, those developments and their related activity have angered retirees and resort owners who see their isolation threatened. Only one year-round resort remains in an area once famous for its saunas and mud baths; a transcendental meditation clinic has replaced another; and anonymous bomb threats periodically force tightened security at geothermal sites.

Overlooking The Geysers from the south is massive Mt. St. Helena (4,343 feet), its sloping table top almost twice as high as the surrounding peaks. Topped now by a lookout tower, the mountain was once an explosive volcano which buried and petrified a forest of gigantic redwoods on its southern flanks. Robert Louis Stevenson honeymooned in an abandoned bunkhouse here in 1880, above the Napa River Valley before it was latticed with vineyards and irrigation tubing. A fire trail still leads to remnants of his cabin and the old Silverado mine.

The mountain was named by the wife of the Governor-General of Russian colonies in America, who scaled the peak in 1841 and claimed to have christened it in honor of St. Helena, the patron saint of the Empress of Russia. The name of the Governor-General's wife, however, may not have been completely immaterial—Helena de Gagarin.

The western section of the North Coast Ranges

Seen from Knights Valley in the Mayacamas Mountains, Mt. St. Helena (left) appears to have been formed by a simple volcano. But though it is composed largely of volcanic rocks, Mt. St. Helena is actually the dismembered, eroded rubble of ancient volcanoes which have long since disappeared. LARRY ULRICH

Beach pea (right), blossoming with pink and white bonnets in Redwood National Park, flourishes in the wettest of the Coast Ranges but does not grow south of Monterey County. RENE PAULI

Big Tree in Prairie Creek Redwoods State Park (far right) is a magnificent specimen of the coastal redwood. These trees, the earth's tallest, grow just out of reach of salt spray and salt-laden winds but not so far inland that they are deprived of thick and frequent fogs which sustain them through California's dry summer months.
LARRY ULRICH

generally consists of lower elevations than the east fork. Along the coast and south to smooth mountain ridges overlooking Bodega Bay, sheep graze with some of the grandest views in the world. A number of North Coast Range ranchers, here and elsewhere, first switched to sheep from cattle during World War II, when wartime lights-out regulations interfered with early-morning milkings.

Mt. Tamalpais, dominating the Marin County skyline just north of San Francisco, is one of four major peaks surrounding the Bay Area. The other three are Mt. St. Helena and, in the South Coast Ranges, Mt. Diablo (3,849 feet) and Mt. Hamilton (4,213 feet). Bay Area Boy Scouts earn merit badges for climbing "the Big Four" peaks.

Interestingly, the highest peak of Mt. Tamalpais was not always its highest. Before World War II, West Peak was actually higher—at an elevation of 2,604 feet—but construction of an Air Force radar base there required that it be flattened and East Peak (2,571 feet) became the highest by default.

The view from Gardiner Lookout atop Mt. Tamalpais is deservedly famous. To the south the top of the Golden Gate Bridge and the city of San Francisco, dwarfed by even the smallest foothills; to the north, the criss-crossing ridges of North Coast Ranges; to the east, San Francisco Bay and, when the air is clear, the Sierra Nevada, almost two hundred miles away; to the west, the ocean and the Farallon Islands where in the 1850s more than 120,000 seabird eggs were gathered in two days and sold by an egg company for a dollar a dozen in thriving but egg-poor San Francisco.

At times, the view *of* Mt. Tamalpais is as breathtaking as the views from it. More than a hundred different species of wildflowers, including blue lupine, poppies, Douglas iris, and blue-eyed grass splash the open mountainsides with color throughout the year, but they are especially dazzling in March and April, when roads are crowded with admirers. Grassfires can make subsequent blooms spectacular, the perfume of the flowers so strong that even sightseers without allergies

Not all mountain wildlife is large and rugged. Some, like the mourning dove, is small and delicate.
WILLIAM HELSEL

develop sneezing and red eyes.

Before the turn of the century, "the crookedest railroad in the world" was built from Mill Valley, two miles and 361 curves away, to a two-story tavern and dance pavillion just below the peak. From here, a "gravity car"—an open free-rolling railroad car with only a brakeman—sped at twenty miles an hour for several miles downhill, through fir forests, chaparral-covered knobs, oak woodlands, and grassy slopes to canyons lush with ferns, trilliums, and coastal redwoods. Hikers follow those old railroad trails through the same

diverse scenery today.

When the North Coast Ranges end abruptly here at Mt. Tamalpais and San Francisco Bay, it is—as usual—with great relief. They have proven that mountains need not be especially high to have their heads in the clouds (or fog, or steam), and that mountainsides need not be especially solid to be steep. They have proven that the tallest peaks don't necessarily get the most rain or grow the tallest trees. The North Coast Ranges have proven, in their way, to be California's most optimistic mountains.

Mt. Morrison (left) and Laurel Mountain (right) of the eastern Sierra Nevada. How did they get their names?
MICHAEL S. SAMPLE

Who names the mountains?

Want to name a peak after your Uncle Hooter?

There are literally thousands of officially unnamed mountain peaks in California. Many are known by local names, many by several names, and many are not known at all.

Thanks to the U.S. Board of Geographic Names and its California Advisory Committee, however, any peak—even your Mt. Hooter—can be officially named. But it's not quite as easy to name Uncle Hooter's mountain as it was to name Uncle Hooter. First you must fill out a Proposal of Name for an Unnamed Domestic Feature, providing such information as the proposed name, a description of the mountain, and its exact latitude and longitude.

The Advisory Committee, representing six state agencies, has different criteria for approving three types of mountain names—major, secondary, and minor mountains. In all three, Uncle Hooter must have died—at least a year ago if your target is a major or secondary one. It also helps if the proposed name is locally used and supported, and if local groups (such as law enforcement, emergency medical, or flight agencies) can demonstrate a need for a name.

But if the peak you want to name Mt. Hooter is a major feature—a whole range; a cluster of high, spectacular peaks; a large ridge; or even an outstanding smaller peak—then you will have to prove that Uncle Hooter was a man of enduring fame (not notoriety), that he rendered public service not merely regional in nature, that the name is clearly supported by local residents, and that no other major feature has been named for him. The Advisory Committee wants to make sure that the importance of Uncle Hooter is commensurate with the peak.

If the proposed Mt. Hooter is a secondary feature—a less remarkable peak in relation to its surroundings, for example, or a small ridge—then you will have to prove that Uncle Hooter was clearly associated with "his" mountain in some way. Here, the Advisory Committee gives marked preference to state servants and members of the Armed Forces who died in the line of duty.

And if, instead of a Mt. Hooter, you simply want to honor your uncle by naming Hooter Hill or some other minor mountain, then you need only show he has died (even if it was only yesterday) and that the name is not distasteful to local residents. If Uncle Hooter was an early occupant or owner of the feature, or if he died in the line of duty, his odds are greatly improved. But don't expect approval of Hooter Mound, since a feature to be considered must at least show up on 7.5-minute USGS quadrangle maps.

Overall, it's harder to gain approval for a peak inside a wilderness area than outside. And if your proposed name is abbreviated, hyphenated, derogatory, or consists of more than one word, it is at a disadvantage.

If the Advisory Committee approves your proposal, they forward it to the national board in Reston, Virginia, which (perhaps because it is so close to Washington, D.C.) does not always rubber stamp or reject applications in accordance with the committee's recommendation. Even if Mt. Hooter does become an official name, it probably won't appear until years later, when the relevant maps are revised—by which time your name, too, may have become eligible.

For further information or application forms, contact any of the following state agencies: State Lands Commission, California Dept. of Water Resources, California Dept. of Forestry, California Dept. of Fish and Game, California Dept. of Parks and Recreation, California Division of Mines and Geology.

Distances diminished

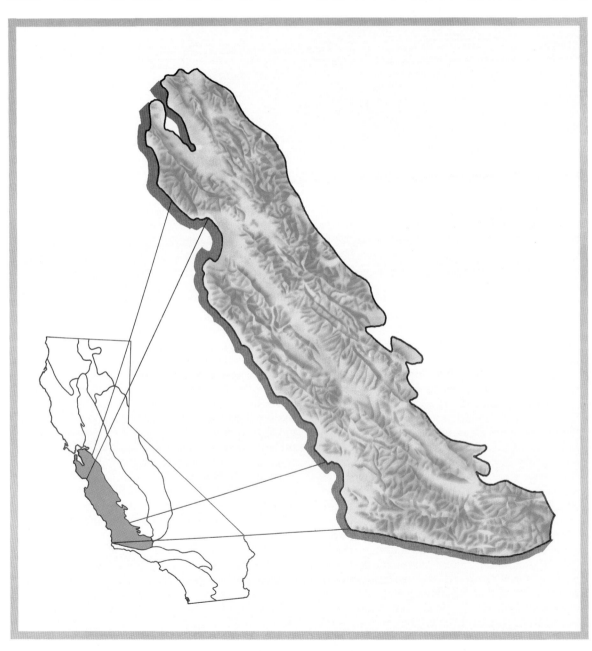

Miles shrink in California's South Coast Ranges. Surveyors have plotted other states from here, and astronomers have plotted other galaxies. Exotic wildlife from all corners of the globe roam these mountains as if they were native. And California condors, having once soared above the continent from Florida to Canada to Mexico, have built the last nests of their species here in areas measured by acres, not miles.

California's South Coast Ranges, more clearly distinguished from each other than their often-jumbled counterparts north of San Francisco Bay, stretch in well-defined and parallel ridges until they merge in confusion with the Transverse Ranges. The South Coast Ranges are dominated by the Santa Lucia Range fronting the coast, but also include major ranges in the Santa Cruz, Diablo, Temblor, and Sierra Madre mountains, as well as smaller ranges such as the Gabilans, Sierra de Salinas, and La Panzas.

Far more exposed than better-dressed mountains to the north, the South Coast Ranges rely on different charms. Dense timber does not interfere as often with the flirting shadows of clouds—captivating, wholly unpredictable, moving in fits and starts from one pale brown ridge to the next. Interlacing fingers of gray-green valley oaks wind through gentle canyons, meeting and parting.

The northernmost peak of significance in the South Coast Ranges also just happens to be the second-most visible peak on earth. The view from Mount Diablo, with an elevation of only 3,849 feet, encompasses more than 40,000 square miles. The peak essentially stands alone on the edge of the great Central Valley. Only Africa's Mt. Kilimanjaro, five times higher, surveys more.

Bay Area fogs, smog, and the smoke from

The Santa Lucia Range plunges into the Pacific Ocean south of Monterey, creating one of the most famous coastlines in the world. JEFF GNASS

smudge pots in valley orchards below often reduce visibility drastically. But evening after evening, tailgate parties and family picnics on the west side of the mountain testify to the dependable popularity of the sunset here, perfectly framed by the Golden Gate Bridge.

From the stone observation platform atop Mount Diablo, the Sutter Buttes and Lassen Peak, 185 miles to the north, are unmistakable. So is Mt. St. Helena. And Mt. Shasta, more than 200 miles north, is also visible—as a partial image of the peak, refracted by the earth's atmosphere.

To the east swells the Sierra Nevada, and trained eyes can even distinguish Half Dome in Yosemite Valley. To the south, reflections glint from Lick Observatory on Mt. Hamilton (4,209 feet), and to the west are Mt. Loma Prieta (elev. 3,791 feet) and other Santa Cruz mountains, creased and stark.

Little wonder that, for 5,000 years, Miwok Indians and their ancestors believed Mount Diablo was the home of deities such as the eagle and the coyote and worshipped the mountain as the birthplace of man. Little wonder, too, that the

peak was quickly chosen in 1851 as the reference point from which to survey the northern two-thirds of California and parts of Oregon and Nevada.

Inside the summit building, an octagonal concrete pillar encasing a copper bolt tapers up through the wooden roof. Here intersect the two most important survey lines in the state, the Mount Diablo Base and Meridian Lines. Near the pillar, a crust of rough rock protrudes through the floor. This is the actual top of Mount Diablo, from which thousands of people every year jump to the

The grand views from California's Santa Lucia Range include not only deep canyons, sparkling ribbons of water, and other peaks at the horizon, but also the stunning Pacific Ocean, which dwarfs even these incomparable mountains. Here backpackers thread their way along slopes in the Ventana Wilderness, more than 160,000 acres in the heart of the Santa Lucias and criss-crossed by 200 miles of trails.
GEORGE WUERTHNER

smooth concrete inches below—thus earning the right to brag about leaping off Mount Diablo.

Mount Diablo itself is a dry hodgepodge of oak woodland, grassland, and chaparral, and on its lower north slopes supports the northernmost stand of Coulter pine. Hang gliders, more daring than those thousands of visitors who leap from the top of the mountain, launch themselves into space from lower elevations, at Gibraltar Rock or Watson Towers. The wind continues to carve caves in the brown boulders here, creating rock skulls full of eyeholes and moaning mouth cavities. Fossil remains of mastodon and saber-toothed tiger have been unearthed on the lower slopes, where maple and dove lupine grow.

As the Diablo Range continues south from Mount Diablo, the valley of Arroyo Mocho skirts Eylar Mountain (4,089 feet) and gives way to Del Puerto Canyon, winding up from the east. Narrow roads following the two canyons merge, and proceed to the summit of Mt. Hamilton, the highest peak in the northern Diablo Range and the highest road summit in the Bay Area. Yosemite's Half Dome is visible among other Sierra peaks from here.

This is the site of the University of California's white-domed James Lick Observatory, home of the world's second-largest reflector telescope. (Mt. Palomar Observatory in the Peninsular Ranges has the largest.) There are other, smaller domes here as well, and a swimming pool, and a garage-sized fire station, and a tiny school for the children of scientists. Signs read: "Quiet please—day sleeper."

Inside the main observatory, the body of James

The rugged Big Sur coastline of the Santa Lucia Range evidences the most visible difference between the North Coast and South Coast ranges. North of San Francisco, coastal slopes are lush with vegetation, but here they maintain a much drier, more barren character. LARRY ULRICH

Lick, namesake and first benefactor of the facility, is buried in the base of the 36-inch telescope which he commissioned. The telescope was the largest in the world when presented, in 1895. This was also the first major observatory located on a mountaintop, isolated far more in those pre-automobile days than it is now, but it quickly proved so successful that virtually all subsequent observatories were similarly sited.

Of course, the great advantage of its mountaintop site is clear air and dark skies. But the increasing light and smog rising from cities growing below have begun to hamper astronomical observations atop Mt. Hamilton. The city of San Jose has recently agreed to cooperate with Lick Observatory to reduce such interference. New subdivisions, for instance, must replace conventional outdoor lighting with low-pressure sodium vapor lamps so that astronomers can filter out the light.

East of the observatory and the crest of the Diablo Range, the San Joaquin Valley below is segregated—dry forests of wind generator towers and propellers suddenly abut irrigated orange and almond groves, where the trunks of trees are taped white like the ankles of racehorses to repel insects. On this side of the Diablos, the hot, barren mountains shimmer with summer heat, cut into deep seams by infrequent thunderstorm rains as if they had been furrowed with a giant rake. The ribs of cattle here show the same deep furrows. There are no fences in these mountains—just metal gates across the roads. Only the frequency and low altitude of commercial airplanes are evidence that nearly two million people live nearby.

Tiny creekbed ponds, scummed over and surrounded by cattails, are the oases here, except for Frank Raines Park, a gorgeous green Del Puerto Canyon meadow complete with stone walls, stone walkways, and even swingsets.

West of Mt. Hamilton, however, the Diablo Range sinks quickly through taller grasses, pines, and scattered cedars into the apricot orchards of the Santa Clara Valley and San Jose. Across that

valley, the eastern foothills of the Santa Cruz Mountains beneath Mt. Loma Prieta are honeycombed with more than a hundred miles of mining tunnels, spawned a quarter century before the 1848 discovery of gold at Sutter's Mill in the Sierra. Three mines near New Almaden exploited deep-red earth for quicksilver, and eventually produced more than $50 million worth of the mercury necessary for gold processing.

John Steinbeck's arid mountains, the Gabilan Range, rise south of the Santa Cruz Mountains, paralleling the Diablo Range to the east and the Santa Lucias to the west. As a boy he often climbed Fremont Peak (3,171 feet) above Salinas, the highest point for miles, and found cannonballs and rusted bayonets where Gen. John C. Fremont made his stand against the Mexican Army and defeated it. As a novelist, Steinbeck described the

Near the Oakland suburb of Livermore, the giant but gentle hills of the South Coast Ranges (above) become a vibrant green each spring.
JAMES RANDKLEV

The rugged San Rafael Mountains (opposite page) present ridge after ridge of chaparral-covered slopes. DAVID MUENCH

view: "The peak overlooks the whole of the Salinas Valley, stretching nearly a hundred miles, the town of Salinas now spreading like crabgrass into the foothills below. Mt. Toro on the brother range to the west was a rounded, benign mountain; and to the north, Monterey Bay shone like a blue platter. I felt and smelled and heard the wind blow up from the long valley—it smelled of the brown hills of wild oats."

On the bald, western edge of the Gabilans, near Soledad, the spires of The Pinnacles rise 1,200 feet above the canyon floors, the last splinters of a volcanic mountain. Chartered hot air balloons float below Fremont Peak now, but lower still the Mexican farm workers harvest lettuce much as they did in Steinbeck's day, by hand, their faces covered with bandanas because of insecticides.

Steinbeck's "brother range to the west," the Sierra de Salinas, stretches south from Mt. Toro (3,560 feet), over Palo Escrito Peak (4,467 feet) in the middle of the range, to Arroyo Seco Canyon. If the ranges are brothers, though, they certainly aren't twins. At lower elevations of their west slopes, especially in the north, the rolling, grassy hills and white-dirt-sided creek banks of the Sierra de Salinas give way to narrow, flat-floored bottomlands crowded with valley and blue oaks, Fremont cottonwoods, and big-leaf maples. Joggers and bicyclists become more frequent. This is the famous Carmel Valley, where palms and Australian eucalyptus border white sand traps on incredibly lush canyon golf courses, where even a doghouse here and there is protected by a colorful golfer's umbrella.

Between the Sierra de Salinas and the Santa Lucias, the town of Carmel insists on remaining a quaint, but incredibly affluent, coast village. Auto parts stores are as carefully sculpted as restaurants, with arches and balconies. Except in the center of town, there are no streetlights, stoplights, sidewalks, or curbs. Houses have no street numbers, because there is no mail delivery. Residents get their own mail at the post office.

The Santa Lucia Mountains, still referred to by some old-timers as the Big Sur Hills, stretch southward from California's first capital, Monterey, to the Cuyama River and Twitchell Reservoir in the south. Fortunate hikers in the Santa Lucias can hear the barking of sea lions and spy the white eruptions of gray whales migrating offshore. California 1, laboriously constructed with the aid of convict labor and perhaps the most celebrated highway in the world, clings desperately to the Santa Lucias just above the crashing surf, terrified of falling.

Sometimes the coast highway does fall, pushed from inland by massive mountainslides. Smaller slides merely wash across the highway, blocking traffic until bulldozers can scrape the loose dirt aside.

Coastal blacktail deer hide here in the rugged 250,000-acre Ventana Wilderness, presided over by Ventana Double Cone (4,853 feet). Mountain lions and a few black bears also roam the backcountry. Timber (which remains uncut because of steep terrain and thin, erosive soils) consists of Monterey, Coulter, digger, and ponderosa pines as well as Santa Lucia firs. Oak, pinyon, and juniper thickets dominate the eastern mountainsides, except at the highest elevations where Santa Lucia and white fir grows. Here, too, California buckeye trees produce smooth, pear-shaped seeds as large as tennis balls.

The tallest peak in the northern Santa Lucias is Junipero Serra Peak (5,862 feet) barely beyond the borders of the Ventana Wilderness. To the south, Cone Peak (5,155 feet) is also just outside the wilderness boundaries. From here, elevations gradually lessen beyond the Hearst Castle, which sprawls magnificently on 123 acres of the Santa Lucias at San Simeon, near Pine Mountain (3,594 feet). Wild boar— introduced from Europe by early settlers and then later by the Hearst estate at San Simeon—now roam the mountains at will and rototill the gardens of residents free of charge. Other Hearst imports which have escaped to populate the Santa Lucias include Rocky Mountain elk, tahr (shaggy, curved-horned goats from Asia), and Barbary sheep.

Inland from the crest of the Santa Lucias, the Hunter Ligget Military Reservation descends to occupy the flat grasslands of the San Antonio River. Not far from rows of military tents and rows of military tanks, old tin-and-plywood guard stations have been converted to deer blinds. Instead of the pulverized rock and precipitous inclines of the western and higher mountains, these smooth and grassy foothills are characterized by huge oaks—knobby, twisted, naked limbs writhing from their trunks like the heads of dragons.

Near San Luis Obispo, the Santa Lucias lose their identity and two smaller ranges take shape—the La Panza Range to the east and the Sierra Madre Mountains to the south. Dividing the two is the Cuyama Valley and the Cuyama River, supporting a few irrigated alfalfa fields along the dry, rust-red riverbed.

Fierce winds funneled between the two ranges and a third, the Caliente Range, have punished the Cuyama Valley. A metal water tank that toppled from its tower years ago now rests against a dry cattle trough hundreds of yards away, crumpled like an empty bean can. Clapboard shacks have been sandblasted clean of paint. Clumsy mobile homes take shelter behind the crumbling walls of adobe houses—even houses, it seems, must be aerodynamically designed here to withstand the winds. And it is so dry that local ranchers are accustomed to driving in dust storms with their windshield wipers on—because it's also raining.

Caliente Mountain (5,106 feet) towers above New Cuyama. Like every other mountain facing the valley, its inhospitable valleys are dark not with trees but merely with shadows. Yet oilfield rocking horses that nod nearby, and countless pickups carrying dirt bikes and three-wheelers, are proof that these harsh ranges have their own attractions.

West of McPherson Peak (5,749 feet) in the

erosive Sierra Madre Mountains, looking away from the Cuyama River, avalanches of brown and red and yellow leaves reach sheer canyon walls and drift like snowflakes into cold streams. But above the occasional shady cottonwood and sycamore thickets, bare Sierra Madre ridges break the surface and send scrub oak and chaparral streaming down their sides in dark green strands and trickles. Boulder fields and talus slopes predominate.

The Sierra Madres and the San Rafael Mountains to their southwest are both included in the 150,000-acre San Rafael Wilderness, which in 1968 became the first Primitive Area to be officially and permanently designated a part of the National Wilderness System. Dominant peaks of the latter range include San Rafael Mountain (6,593 feet) and Big Pine Mountain (6,828 feet), both within the wilderness. The wilderness also contains the 1,200-acre Sisquoc condor sanctuary, one of the last known nesting sites of the rare bird and closed at all times. Other portions of the San Rafael Wilderness are regularly closed during summer and autumn because of extreme fire danger.

The last band of significant mountains of the South Coast Ranges, the Temblors, form a thin buffer of peaks and ridges for nearly a hundred miles between the great San Joaquin Valley and the rest of the South Coast Ranges south of the Diablos. The highest peaks in the Temblors include McKittrick Summit (4,332 feet) and Midway Peak (3,362 feet), both in the southern half of the range.

From here, as from so many other South Coast Ranges peaks, miles seem almost irrelevant. Vast views transform the San Joaquin Valley into an immense ocean where strong winds bounce tumbleweeds as large as beach balls across the lush green waves of irrigated wheat, barley, and cotton. The far slopes of valleys, the far shores of continents, the distant past of stars—all come equally within reach in the South Coast Ranges.

Luxuriant valley lupine billows across the rolling hills of the Carmel Valley in the South Coast Ranges. CARR CLIFTON

Going against the grain

In a state where every major mountain range trends southeast-northwest, the Transverse Ranges and the Tehachapis go against the grain. The Santa Ynez, Santa Monica, San Gabriel, and San Bernardino mountains all exhibit east-west orientations. So, too, do the Little San Bernardino mountains, although less prominently. And the Tehachapis (not strictly a Transverse Range, although quite similar) form a southwest-northeast link between these ranges and the Sierra Nevada.

Excluding the Santa Monicas, these ranges are the most rugged and sparsely settled mountain province along the California coast. They climb steadily from west to east. The San Andreas Fault, partly responsible for their unusual alignment,

separates the San Gabriels and San Bernardinos, and in fact, some geologists believe the two ranges were once one. The Transverse Ranges are rising, too, another result of the collision of earth crusts which has pinched these mountains between the South Coast Ranges to the north and the Peninsular Ranges to the south.

The Santa Ynez Mountains, extending from Point Concepcion to Lake Casitas and the Ventura River, claim White Ledge Peak (4,640 feet) in the east as their dominant peak. The majority of the range is included within Los Padres National Forest.

Like the Sierra Madres and San Rafaels to the north, the chaparral-covered slopes of the Santa Ynez Mountains are vulnerable to fire. Mountain-

side after mountainside passes the winter in black, thickening the air for miles with the smell of wet charcoal. Rainwater runs black beside the road, and into pools, turning white sand in the streambeds a charred black.

Thanks to the Santa Monica Mountains, people throughout the world who have never visited

Seen from Saddleback Butte State Park where Joshua trees are numerous and striking, the San Gabriel Mountains to the west show no hint of the dense population and intense development in Los Angeles just beyond. ED COOPER

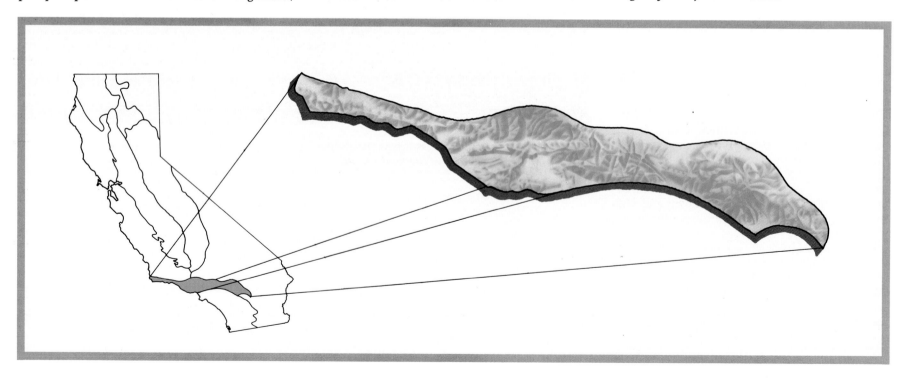

California know what the Transverse Ranges look like. These mountains southeast of the Santa Ynez range look exactly like those in Korea—at least as portrayed in the television series M*A*S*H, which filmed all its outdoor scenes at Malibu State Park.

The Santa Monicas, shortest of the Transverse Ranges, have been affected by water more than fire. They actually extend far into the Pacific Ocean, and some geologists consider the islands of Santa Cruz, Santa Rosa, and San Miguel to be Santa Monica peaks. But since most Californians are not geologists, the Channel Islands remain a breed apart.

Though small, the Santa Monicas contain some near-wilderness areas, consisting mainly of dense brushlands which stretch east to separate the Los Angeles Basin from the San Fernando Valley. The 40,000-acre Santa Monica Mountains National Recreation Area became one of California's major casualties in the battle against government deficits when, in 1981, Interior Secretary James Watt achieved $14.7 million in budget cuts mostly by cancelling $14.2 million of land purchases for the area. Not surprisingly, real estate developers have stepped in, casting doubt on expansion of the recreation area in the future.

The largest city park in the nation, Los Angeles' 4,000-acre Griffith Park, is located just east of the Santa Monica Mountains on the Los Angeles River. Arid and mountainous, its aerial views of the city are more popular with motorists than hikers or strollers.

The Tehachapi Mountains, geologically the southernmost extension of the Sierra, are in most other respects—topography, trend, politics—more similar to the Transverse Ranges. They are reknowned chiefly as the hurdle to be crossed between Los Angeles and points north. Rich, chocolate-brown fields look as if they are attempting the crossing, venturing up from the flat San Joaquin Valley and into the barren foothills, rippling at the edges like flounders. Above them, Double Mountain (7,981 feet), at the north end of the Tehachapis, is the tallest peak in the range.

The most spectacular crossing of that hurdle was undoubtedly the 1876 completion of the Tehachapi Loop, one of the most remarkable feats of railroad engineering of its time. Faced with a steep, half-mile incline in the short distance between Caliente and Tehachapi, the railroad makes a complete circle of 3,795 feet and uses the maximum gradients and tightest curves possible. The tracks wind a total of twenty-eight miles, through seventeen sooty tunnels visible from the highway, to travel fourteen miles between the two towns.

Another crossing of the Tehachapis, this one by water, remains the greatest accomplishment of its kind. State Water Project water, flowing from the San Joaquin Valley in the California Aqueduct, must be lifted 2,000 feet by pumps and tunneled beneath the Tehachapis before it can flow down the southern slopes of the Tehachapis to Los Angeles and San Diego. The crossing requires that more water be pumped higher than anywhere else in the world.

The strategic location of the Tehachapis had prompted the federal government to establish Fort Tejon there twenty-two years earlier, in 1854, north of Tejon Pass. Now an historical monument with displays, artifacts, and oak-shaded picnic tables, the fort once was home to the U.S. Army Camel Corps. Despite their obvious advantages for carrying supplies to isolated desert outposts, however, the camels proved to be tenderfoots—their hooves could not withstand the rocky soil of the Tehachapis. The experiment was abandoned.

Without a clearly defined range, or even ridge,

Helping nature on the ski slopes

In the Transverse Ranges, snow skiers are more dependable than snow is. As a result, winter resorts such as those at Big Bear Lake must try harder.

To begin with, ski resorts in Southern California must cut trees differently when first clearing their slopes. Unlike Sierra resorts, where snows four feet deep and more cover tree stumps, resorts in the San Gabriels and San Bernardinos sometimes get as little as 6-8 inches of snow. Consequently, trees must either be flush-cut (by digging a trench and using a chainsaw below ground level) or pulled completely from the ground.

And because both skiers and the "snow cats" which groom these slopes are constantly pushing snow downhill, even snow two feet deep may not last long. So ski resorts in the Transverse Ranges rely heavily on snow machines and "Oreo-cookie skiing"— white in the middle, brown at the edges.

Ski area operators are correct when they insist that "it's not artificial snow, it's machine-made snow." Coming from separate hoses, compressed air and water are forced together in a snow gun, which sprays a fine mist into the air. But despite all the expensive machinery, it's the air—and the right combination of temperature and humidity—which turns the mist to snow. Even when temperatures reach 40 degrees Fahrenheit, it's possible to make snow providing humidity is less than thirty percent. On the other hand, high humidity can render snow machines impotent even when temperatures are below freezing.

The resulting "fried" snow is often crunchier, louder, tougher—and faster—than what falls from the sky, and skiing on it becomes an art. In fact, skiers who learn and survive on artificial snow are among the best in the world.

in the area where the Tehachapis and Transverse Ranges mingle, the dominant peak has lent its name to the region. Mt. Pinos (8,831 feet) is the pebble pinched in the giant lobster claw of California mountains, between the Sierra and the Coast Ranges. Although its bare summit, topped by a microwave station, is a few feet south of the boundary between Kern and Ventura counties, Mt. Pinos nevertheless enjoys the distinction of being the highest peak in both counties. From this and other peaks in the Mt. Pinos region, the last condors surviving in the wild are occasionally spotted effortlessly soaring on warm, early-afternoon updrafts.

Although the San Gabriel Mountains were named "Sierra de San Gabriel" as early as 1776, that name had competition. Spanish padres referred to the peaks as the Sierra Madres, a name which gained wide acceptance in an era when travel was slow, contact between settlements was minimal, and mountain ranges were worlds apart. But by the twentieth century, when new modes of transportation, communication, and commerce had begun to shrink distances, USGS had assigned the former name to avoid confusion with the Sierra Madres to the northwest. Long-time residents were furious and protested loudly, but in 1927 the U.S. Board of Geographic Names made it official.

John Muir called the San Gabriel Mountains "more rigidly inaccessible than any other I ever attempted to penetrate." Unlike other Transverse Ranges, the San Gabriels are often more abrupt on their seaward (south) slopes than on their inland (north) slopes, due to massive faulting and uplifts—tilting— caused as they are squeezed between the South Coast and Peninsular ranges. Cucamonga Peak (8,859 feet), for example, rises 7,000 feet northward from the valley in about five miles. Desert valleys to the north of the San Gabriels are generally higher in elevation, so relief is not as great.

Big Tujunga Canyon and the San Gabriel River

Beavertail cactus ekes out a precarious yet beautiful existence on a rock cliff in the Little San Bernardino Mountains. PATTY A. FURBUSH

valley join to rupture the San Gabriels into parallel crests, with the tallest peaks to the north exceeding 8,000 and 9,000 feet. Grandest of these, of course, is Mt. San Antonio, locally known as Old Baldy (10,064 feet) at the blunt eastern end of the range. Steep trails, thin air, and frequent glazes of snow make this perhaps the most treacherous climb in the Transverse Ranges—in one particularly deadly week, four people died in separate falls.

The San Gabriels are the heart of 700,000-acre Angeles National Forest, more than 36,000 acres of that comprising the San Gabriel Wilderness. The Angeles Crest Highway (California 2) runs along much of the San Gabriel Range, and includes a spur road to Mt. Wilson (5,710 feet), where the Mount Wilson Observatory has become one of the range's most identifiable landmarks. It was here astronomers first realized the universe consists of more than one galaxy. The observatory's celebrated 100-inch telescope was shut down in 1985, however, and visitors are no longer allowed.

These are mountains of many charms besides hiking among dense thickets of chaparral, mature stands of mixed pine, and five-pound Coulter pine cones. The range contains six sizeable ski resorts, the most popular of which are on Thunder Mountain just south of Mt. San Antonio, and at Wrightwood. Additionally, an off-road recreational vehicle area at San Gabriel Reservoir draws thousands of two-, three-, and four-wheelers to roostertail through the sand of dry streambeds.

The Rim-of-the-World Drive (California 18) climbs above an ocean of shopping centers, freeways, and subdivisions to elevations above 7,000 feet as it threads its way across the San Bernardinos, the highest range in Southern California.

Not surprisingly, the partitioned San Bernardino National Forest, 650,000 acres encompassing most of the San Bernardino and San Jacinto mountains, is the most heavily visited national forest in the United States. It is within a two-hour drive of more than 10 million Californians, and records more than 6 million visitor-days per year. Its greatest single attraction is snow skiing.

San Gorgonio Mountain, "Old Greyback" (11,501 feet), is the highest peak in both the San Bernardinos and all of southern California. Like Mt. San Antonio in the San Gabriels, it too towers at the eastern limit of its range. On its north face, steep-walled basins and piles of loose rock—cirques and moraines—testify to the presence of several small, isolated glaciers (perhaps as many as seven) during the last ice age.

The peak is the centerpiece of the San Gorgonio Wilderness, increased in 1984 to 55,000 acres of rock, isolated meadows, and breathtaking vistas. The San Gorgonio Wilderness includes all of the San Bernardino mountains above 10,000 feet.

Just west of San Gorgonio Mountain is San Bernardino Peak (10,649 feet), interesting for two reasons. First, as the reference point for land surveys in southern California, it is the counterpart of Mount Diablo in the South Coast Ranges. Second, the summit which is named San Bernardino Peak and which serves as the reference point for surveyors is actually not the summit at all—the true peak, 359 feet higher, is a half-mile east, but less visible from the valley below.

When the Santa Ana River in the shadow of San Gorgonio Mountain and Sugarloaf Mountain (9,952 feet) was dammed in 1884 to create Big Bear Lake, it marked California's first major use of storage to control surface flow. Until the mid-1970s, the lake was frequently dry enough in summer to walk across, drained for irrigation in the San Bernardino Valley. But agreements between owners of Big Bear property and owners of Big Bear water stabilized water levels.

Now, this beautiful blue lake amid gorgeous forests, ringed by privately owned cabins and (because of underwater springs) rarely frozen, is stocked regularly with rainbow and brown trout to attract anglers. Thousands of off-road vehicles, some driven by preschool children, explore Forest Service roads, create new ones of their own, and hone the emergency medical skills of Forest Ser-

vice personnel. The lake region boasts the world's largest lodgepole pine—110 feet high, with a circumference of 20 feet—and pamphlets publicize the gold mining history of the area (more gold per square mile was taken from nearby Holcomb Valley than anywhere else in southern California). The California Institute of Technology maintains a silver-domed solar observatory here, on a narrow stone promontory jutting into the lake.

Bald eagles also attract visitors. As many as thirty-three of the majestic birds winter here from December to April, watching for fish from trees around Big Bear Lake and occasionally feeding on coots at shallow Baldwin Lake to the east.

But Big Bear is, first and foremost, an oasis of ski resorts above the rocks and deserts of the surrounding region. The south side of the lake alone sports three separate ski areas. Ski shops line the highway, and warm chalets wrap around huge, smooth boulders. Here in the "Arctic Circle" (nicknamed by workers who built the roads and avalanche chutes), snowplows create their own massive white boulders, making way for tens of thousands of weekend skiers.

These mountains can be highly erosive. Mountainslides carry huge boulders and dead wood like driftwood on the crest of a flash flood. A continuously moving mountain mass of 18 million cubic yards threatens the San Gabriel ski resort community of Wrightwood, where the snow is often dusted by loose red dirt from uphill slopes. Elsewhere, heavy rains regularly trigger massive slides known as debris flows. Heavy downpours in the winter of 1978, for example, swept away the town of Hidden Springs in the heart of the San Gabriels and churned thirty bodies from graves in the Verdugo Hills Cemetery, depositing them on the streets and lawns of Tujunga.

The San Gabriels and San Bernardinos suffer from their position high above the Los Angeles Basin, and not simply in terms of heavy use. As they absorb and reflect sunlight, heating the air, the mostly bare southern and western slopes of both ranges pull smog from the basin and 450-square-mile Greater Los Angeles like smoke up a chimney. Once in the mountains, exhaust fumes of 5 million cars a day—fumes which have been irradiated by sunlight into ozone—destroy the photosynthesizing cells of pine needles. Entire stands of big-cone Douglas firs, various pines, white fir, and incense cedars growing on higher and northern slopes become a mottled green, their needles yellowing from the tips back. Ponderosa pines are most severely affected. Smog has diminished harvestable ponderosa pines by half in the San Bernardinos, weakening the trees' resistance to bark beetles and other pests.

Unlike San Francisco, where a gap in the Coast Ranges continually flushes smog east out of the Bay Area, the San Gabriel and San Bernardino mountains act as a barrier. They pull smog upward and toward themselves but also cooler, heavier ocean air into the Los Angeles Basin, where it stubbornly settles and concentrates emissions.

At the eastern edge of the Transverse Ranges, the Little San Bernardino Mountains spread into desert terrain more typical of the Basin Ranges. From Salton View (5,185 feet), the sweep of scenery is astounding. To the west of the Salton Sea (-235 feet), the Peninsular Ranges climb more than 11,000 feet in forty miles, culminating in San Jacinto Peak. Brief glints of sunlight track automobiles making their way through the ocean of gray-green chaparral between the two ranges.

The Little San Bernardinos also resemble a Basin Range in their alignment—more northwest-southeast than other Transverse Ranges and thus, more typical of mountain ranges in California. Even among themselves, it seems, the Transverse Ranges go against the grain.

This Antelope Valley hillside is a celebration of color—yellow goldfields, orange California poppies, and purple owl's clover. JAMES RANDKLEV

Between ocean and desert

California's Peninsular Ranges resume the dominant southeast-northwest trend of mountains that is interrupted by the Transverse Ranges immediately north. The Santa Ana, San Jacinto, and Santa Rosa mountain chains are the longest and most distinct here, all in the northern section of the region. Farther toward the Mexican border, the Peninsular Ranges mingle together more, making it difficult to tell where one ends and another begins.

The Peninsular Ranges are characterized throughout by small valleys, upland plains, and rocky plateaus. Inclines tend to be significantly steeper on the eastern, inland slopes due to faulting. The large numbers of California fan palms along the eastern edge of the San Jacinto and Santa Rosa mountains, for instance, are attributable to the same faults, where underground water is dammed and forced toward the surface by the break.

As the destination for a tide of recreational vehicles, jeeps, and off-road vehicles flowing out of the Los Angeles area every Friday afternoon and then ebbing from the mountains Sunday night, the Peninsular Ranges compete with the Transverse Ranges as the most popular mountain getaways for Southern Californians. And as geographic features, the Peninsular Ranges actually extend south of the California-Mexico border and to the tip of Baja California, making them a longer chain of mountains than even the much-heralded Sierra Nevada.

The Santa Ana Mountains, most northern and western of the Peninsular Ranges, are contained within the Cleveland National Forest's Trabuco Ranger District. (The forest has two other sizeable districts in the Peninsular Ranges, and all three are widely separated.) The Santa Anas reach their pin-

April brings wildflowers to bloom near West Palm Springs, but the upper slopes of Mt. San Jacinto—highest peak in the Peninsular Ranges—are still mantled with deep snow. ED COOPER

nacle at Santiago Peak (5,687 feet), which stands isolated from other major peaks and so is quite visible—and quite useful, judging by more than 125 radio, TV, and microwave facilities at its summit. Not surprisingly, a road leads there.

Yet most visitors from the Los Angeles area see the Santa Ana Mountains not from here but from the south, in and above the winding San Juan and San Mateo canyons, which collect thick white clouds from the ocean and vent them upward like steam. Nearly 30,000 acres along the latter canyon have been proposed for wilderness status.

The San Jacinto Mountains are generally taller in the north, where towering San Jacinto Peak (10,804 feet) faces San Gorgonio in the San Bernardino Mountains. Between the two peaks and their respective ranges, deep San Gorgonio Pass often funnels brownish yellow smog from the Los Angeles Basin into the upper Coachella Valley, obscuring Palm Springs at the foot of San Jacinto Peak.

The rise between the pass and the peak, within a horizontal distance of less than six miles, makes this one of the greatest escarpments on the continent. The San Jacintos as a whole segregate the orchards and wheat fields of the San Jacinto Valley to the west from Palm Springs and the scorching desert floor of the Coachella Valley to the east, where date palms thrive in a climate hotter than Libya's, averaging 106 degrees Fahrenheit every day in July.

In less than eighteen minutes, the "eighth engineering masterpiece of the world," the Palm Springs Aerial Tramway, can levitate heat-weary riders eight thousand feet above Palm Springs to the lingering snows of Mt. San Jacinto and the 13,000-acre Mt. San Jacinto State Park nearby, where snowshoes and cross-country skis are for rent. The 2.5-mile journey along cables slung through Chino Canyon offers spectacular scenery and drops in temperature of 30-40 degrees.

Also nearby, perched incredibly on an eastern ridge, is Bob Hope's house, larger than many

department stores. On the other side of the mountain, Idyllwild, at the southwest edge of the park, is the only genuinely "alpine" settlement in the entire Peninsular Ranges, even hosting dogsled races each winter.

Scorching though it may be on most of the desert floor below Mt. San Jacinto, there are more than forty golf courses within a twenty-mile radius of Palm Springs. Seen from the mountains, their lush fairways and stately palms—like the green lawns and white houses of Palm Springs itself—are geometric patterns, neat angles and straight edges beseiged by bare dirt and rocks. Rorschach blots of white sand traps do little to resolve the conflict.

In places here, knobs and ridges and even whole mountains seem to be nothing but overwhelming rock piles, acres of round, smooth, rust-red boulders piled so deep that not even hardy chaparral can survive. Standing just within the San Jacinto Wilderness is Tahquitz Peak (8,823 feet), a shoulder of Mt. San Jacinto. Now topped by a fire lookout tower, Tahquitz was once feared by the Cahuilla Indians as the home of an evil and powerful medicine man whose name was given to the mountain.

The crest of the San Jacintos continues southeast, fading into the crest of the Santa Rosa Mountains. But the Garner Valley, Lake Hemet, and the South Fork San Jacinto River separate the crest of the range from another prominent ridge. Between them, in a high, grassy plateau near the town of Anza, cattle graze beneath the white granite outcrop of Thomas Mountain (6,811 feet).

The Santa Rosa Mountains, split from the San Jacintos by the pass misnamed Santa Rosa Summit, drop east into the Anza-Borrego Desert State Park, the largest state park in the nation. Sheer-faced, strewn with boulders, and cut by steep-cliffed canyons, they are next to impassable. The Santa Rosa Mountains State Wilderness, 87,000 acres in the northwest corner of Anza-Borrego, is extremely rugged, with virtually no water to be found. Another 136,000 acres of the mountains im-

mediately north are among the most pristine and spectacular anywhere in California's deserts. Ranked fourth by the Bureau of Land Management among 137 Wilderness Study Areas in California, the proposed wilderness is a stronghold of peninsular bighorn sheep.

The most famous of the interconnected Agua Tibia and Palomar mountains, west of the Santa Rosas, is undoubtedly massive Mt. Palomar (6,140 feet), stretching some twenty miles and home of the largest reflecting telescope in the Western world. The Mount Palomar Observatory houses the 200-inch, 500-ton Hale Telescope, able to peer a billion light years (more or less) into space.

Toward the coast, between Fallbrook and Escondido, irrigated mountain valleys and mesas produce more avocados than are grown anywhere else in California. But such productivity comes at a cost—dams built across mountain streams and canyons not only capture water for irrigation, but they also capture eroded sands that would otherwise replenish California's southern beaches, which are now rapidly shrinking. Even at sea level, it seems, mountains are an integral part of California's landscape.

The western peaks of the Laguna Mountains, sometimes called the San Diego Mountains, are the highest in the southern Peninsular Ranges. Cuyamaca Peak (6,512 feet), on the western boundary of Cuyamaca Rancho State Park, is the tallest, with beautiful views of the Pacific Ocean, Mexico, and the Salton Sea surrounded by desert.

The 24,000-acre park is surprisingly well forested, especially considering the moonscapes to the east. Huge black oaks and canyon live oaks shade the chaparral and grassland of rugged mountainsides, while willows, sycamores, and alders pad the streambeds with yellow leaves in autumn. Toward the top of Cuyamaca Peak, incense cedars and white firs join various pines.

The Peninsular Ranges continue to sink toward the south, posting El Cajon (3,675 feet), Los Pinos (4,805 feet), and San Ysidro (3,572 feet) mountains along the way. At sunrise, steam rises from the trunks of oaks, from fenceposts and wooden signs and wooden cattle ramps clustered in the deepest, shadiest canyons of these and other, unnamed mountains. During the afternoon, bright vapor trails overhead follow close behind streaking Navy jets, evaporating quickly into the dry blue air. And at the Mexican border, nearly a thousand miles of California mountain ranges bordering the ocean suddenly end.

Torrey yucca (right) protects its large yellow petals behind an intimidating burst of sharp spikes. The San Jacinto Mountains loom in the distance. DAVID MUENCH

The Basin Ranges:
Diversity in extremes

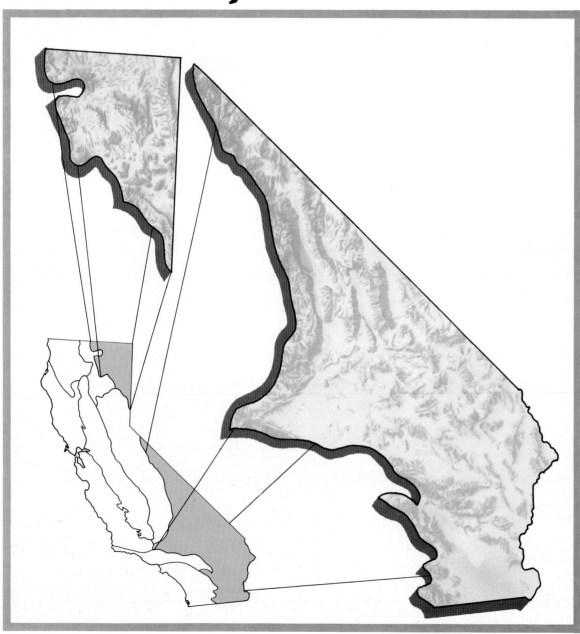

No province of mountains in California includes as many ranges, or as diverse, as the Basin Ranges region. With more than fifty easily distinguished mountain ranges stretching from the southeast to the northeast corners of the state, the Basin Ranges include some of the highest and most foreboding peaks in the state. Some of those peaks erupt from and overlook Death Valley, the lowest and hottest surface on the continent. Others preside over high, frozen plateaus in winter which become (as one aging Modoc County rancher grumbled) "the only place in California where the tap water's so cold it hurts your teeth."

California's Basin Ranges are actually the western edges of a unified, much larger Basin-and-Range landform which extends far east of California. The eastern border of the state, however, splits California's portions of this landform into regions far removed from each other.

In the south, dozens of small, dispersed Basin Ranges (often referred to as the Desert Ranges) extend westward from the Arizona border to include the Chocolate and El Paso mountains. To the north and along the Owens Valley, the ranks of the Basin Ranges include the formidable Inyo and White mountains, giants who do not flinch in the face of the High Sierra arrayed against them. And in extreme northern California, after exiting and reentering the state, the Basin Ranges outflank the Sierra and scatter toward the Cascades, with only one long chain of peaks, the Warner Mountains, maintaining an unbroken profile.

With the exception of the tiny Cargo Muchachos, the southernmost of the Basin Ranges are the Chocolate Mountains, a barren string of low peaks overlooking the Imperial Valley. The perspective

Telescope Peak and Death Valley seem surprisingly close at hand here, seen from Golden Canyon. The steep-walled, narrow canyon was carved through clay and silt which was once a lakebed before faulting raised it into a mountain. LARRY ULRICH

from these peaks is striking—small, square green fields are packed together as densely as if they were silicon chips. The explanation behind checkerboarding on such a small scale lies in the peculiar method of irrigation here, where hundreds of miles of crisscrossing pipes just below the surface carry away used irrigation water and its salts, which otherwise would render the soil useless.

Cottonwood trees and California fan palms cluster around seasonal springs that seep from fractures in these mountains. And growing on the lower slopes of the southern Basin Ranges are two of the most intriguing plants in the entire state. Joshua Trees, sheathed in their own dead spines, climb up to elevations as high as 5,000 feet. Not actually trees but members of the lily family, these yuccas have no cambium rings to permit dating, so estimates of age must be based on their height.

And on mountain hillsides throughout the Colorado Desert, jojoba (also known as goatnut) lives hundreds of years by turning only the edges of its flat leaves to the sun, minimizing both heat and evaporation. Conservationists pin great hopes to these fifteen-foot-high shrubs. The plant's waxy oil is chemically identical to the prized oil of sperm whales, which are being hunted to extinction. The oil also has a mild odor, no toxicity, and extreme purity; it won't dry, turn rancid, or deteriorate after heating. In fact, it is proving perfectly suited to a wide range of uses, from automotive oil to lubricating artificial human hearts.

Although hardly a mountain range, Saddleback Butte Peak (3,651 feet), a jagged mound of granite rising above the Antelope Valley southeast of the Tehachapis, might be considered the westernmost peak of the lower Basin Ranges. The peak offers fine views of the Mojave Desert, much of it planted now in green fields of irrigated alfalfa. Unfortunately, the pronghorn antelope which gave the valley its name have completely disappeared. When railroad lines cut through the valley in 1876, vast herds of seasonally migrating pronghorns

Hikers on the Golden Canyon trail are dwarfed by the stark features of Zabriskie Point and the Black Mountains. In these desert mountains, cool nights bring an almost immeasurable film of moisture to the landscape, nourishing lichens which in turn concentrate minerals such as iron and magnesium, producing a black varnish after many years. TOM BEAN

were psychologically unable to cross the tracks, and were decimated within two years by starvation and severe winters.

Within the immense area between Saddleback Butte and the Nevada border, dust devils a mile high spin furiously, aimlessly, between the heated, rocky walls of rust-red mountains. Here, surrounded by desert basins, huge sheets of blown sand—"climbing dunes"—crawl up the mountainsides until, crossing a ridge, they become falling dunes, huddling in valleys and sinking slowly like glaciers. Sunrise and sunset send the shadows of peaks racing across intervening basins, faster than any man can run, and streak the blue sky with canyons of light. On still, quiet nights, canyons such as those in the western Providence Moun-

tains can echo with the faint booms and bells of shifting "musical dunes," disturbed by the wind or even footsteps. It is the same haunting music recorded by astronauts on the moon.

Perhaps the most awesome sight ever to unfold beneath the summit of Clark Mountain (7,929 feet), the highest Basin Ranges peak south of the Panamints, occurred in 1972, when a motorcycle race between Barstow and Las Vegas churned 600 tons of dust into the air, more than ten times the dust raised by the worst Owens Lakebed dust storms. Thermal currents carried the reddish plume thousands of feet into the atmosphere, high enough to be detected by weather satellites.

The Providence Mountains, named by immigrants thankful for the many springs there, com-

bine with the New York Mountains to form one of the most prominent ridges in southeastern California—fifty miles long, evenly spaced with several peaks higher than 6,000 feet. The Providence Mountains themselves present bold cliffs and buttress-like ridges to the town of Kelso on the west. To the east, winding through creosote bush and volcanic cinders, the dirt trails of longhorns and wild burros and bighorn sheep—all competitors for food—skirt Spotted Horse Mesa (5,028 feet), its sloping top guarded by a stockade fence of black rock. The daylight barks of coyotes are dwarfed by vast, deep, empty spaces between ranges.

Beneath the sun-scorched Providence Mountains are some of California's most famous caves. Mitchell Caverns, three hundred feet deep, contain miles of explored and unexplored tunnels. Their cool limestone rooms are furnished with intricate curtains, pillars, stalactites, and stalagmites, and are surprisingly dry. They were used for centuries by Indians for shelter and food storage.

In the foothills of many Basin Range mountains, especially those surrounding Death Valley, curious mushroom-shaped rocks have been sculpted by blowing sand. The "stalks" of these rocks, sandblasted by heavier grains which winds could not lift very high, erode faster than the grotesquely carved and hollowed "crowns." Eventually, the precarious formation collapses; but until it does, it serves the mountains as an eerie substitute for non-existent vegetation.

Actually, of course, vegetation is not really non-existent. It just seems to be. Hidden springs scattered throughout the Basin Ranges support tiny green oases on the mountainsides. About once every eight years, even the most barren and rocky mountainsides burst into yellow brilliance when

Sunrise breaks across Anza-Borrego Desert State Park. DAVID MUENCH

desert sunflowers take advantage of exceptional rains. Smaller blooms of lupines and other wildflowers occur for a few short weeks every year. Thorny ocotillo stalks lend red flowers; sand dunes become pink with verbena; yuccas sprout huge white plumes. And at higher elevations, such as the upper slopes of the Panamint Range west of Death Valley, forests of pinyon and juniper find enough moisture to survive. Limber and bristlecone pines cling to the very tallest peaks.

Yet even where the Basin Ranges seem most incapable of supporting life, they do. Wild burros, the white-muzzled and rangy descendants of miners' pack animals, roam the lower canyons and foothills of the Panamints. Orange highway signs like those used in other mountains at deer or cattle crossings warn motorists here of wild burro crossings. But the comical black silhouettes of long-eared, round-humped asses on these Basin Ranges signs belie a serious problem. The Bureau of Land Management, claiming that the animals severely damage the Death Valley ecosystem, has removed more than 4,300 of them from the Panamints in the first two years of a three-year relocation program. Yet an estimated 2,000 wild burros remained in 1986, the final year of round-ups, most of them inhabiting the Cottonwood Mountains (a northern sub-range of the Panamints, not to be confused with the sub-range of the Little San Bernardinos which bears the same name).

Telescope Peak (11,049 feet) is the tallest peak in the Panamints. Its magnificent descent straight into Death Valley and Badwater (-282 feet), lowest surface in the western hemisphere, constitutes *the* major escarpment on the continent, nearly a thousand feet greater than the one formed by Mt. Whitney west of the Owens Valley.

The Panamints—like other ranges—flush huge, fan-shaped deposits of rock and soil from their slopes. In places—often below the snowiest peaks—these alluvial fans have become so large that they merge, forming a continuous apron along

The 5,000-acre Picacho State Recreation Area in the Chocolate Mountains, apparently desperate for water, actually has two boat-in camping areas, thanks to about eight miles of Colorado River frontage. CARR CLIFTON

the base of the ranges. Scientists estimate the floor of Death Valley is covered 9,000 feet deep with the earth eroded from surrounding mountains.

Across Death Valley to the east, the Amargosa Range encompasses a number of sub-ranges, including the Black, Greenwater, and Funeral mountains. The Black and Funeral ranges form the eastern escarpment of Death Valley. These ranges exhibit every color of rock imaginable—pale rust red, dirty white, green, mustard yellow, brown, gray, black. Whole mountains jut from the earth, exposing massive layers of rock which swoop upward as gracefully as the concentric swirls of a clamshell.

Despite the inherent attraction of the idea, and regardless of the assurances of hundreds of pages, pamphlets, and books, the highest point in the contiguous United States is not within sight of the lowest. From Dante's View (5,475 feet) on the crest of the Black Mountains, however, both Mt. Whitney and Death Valley *are* visible.

Sediments wash into Death Valley from both the Black and Funeral mountains, just as from the Panamints, but the alluvial fans on this side of the valley are next to invisible. Measurements indicate that the same faulting which produced the surrounding ranges is also tilting Death Valley to the east, actually sinking it beneath the Black Mountains. As a result, valley sediments are sliding east, too, overwhelming and burying the Black Mountains fans.

North of Death Valley, the White and Inyo Mountains are a single massive block 110 miles long. *Average* elevations are around 10,000 feet, with a dozen peaks in the White Mountains rising well above 11,000 feet and half that many in the Inyos. White Mountain Peak (14,242 feet) is the third-highest peak in California and the highest outside of the Sierra.

Here, in a frozen desert comparable to those surrounding the earth's poles, bristlecone pines more than four thousand years old endure punishing wind and cold. Variously regarded as the world's

The Patriarch Grove of bristlecone pines in the White Mountains (above) is one of the most popular groves of the ancient, hardy trees. Because the dense wood of bristlecone pines has unusually small cells, which retard insect damage and decay, it remains intact long after it dies, slowly polished by sand blasts into picturesque snags. LARRY ULRICH

The Wildrose Charcoal Kilns in the Panamint Range (left), still pungent with the smells of resin and creosote, were built in 1877 to manufacture charcoal for use in two nearby smelters. Pinyon pines of the Panamints were "cooked" in the absence of air to produce charcoal, which was then used in smelting silver and lead ores extracted from the nearby Argus Range. LINDA WEEKS

oldest living things, its oldest living trees, or (merely?) one of its most ancient and indestructible surviving inhabitants, bristlecone pines seldom exceed heights of forty feet. They retain their needles for thirty years and more and may remain living in only a narrow strip of weathered bark and a few needles— and still capable of producing seeds even when only ten percent of their tissue still lives.

North of the White Mountains, the high Basin Ranges sink into Mono Valley, where bizarre white limestone pinnacles—tufa towers—and receding terraces—the lake's "bathtub rings"— mark the lowering of Mono Lake (6,400 feet). Although the lake has slowly risen and fallen for centuries, in concert with the freezing and melting of Sierra snow pack and glaciers above, its level recently plunged when mountain feedwaters were diverted south into the Los Angeles Aqueduct. Land bridges emerged in the lake, giving predators access to island nesting sites of California gulls, and concentrated salinity began killing the brine shrimp and flies on which the birds fed. The ensuing controversy and legal battles recently forced Los Angeles to raise the level of Mono Lake slightly and maintain it there, a requirement which is not expected to hit Los Angeles with full force until the next statewide drought.

After exiting California near Mono Lake, the Basin Ranges reenter the state in the northeast corner, in the Pit River country known as the Modoc Plateau. Many of these ranges are geologically related to the volcanic Cascade Range to the west, and they exhibit a split personality when compared to Basin Ranges farther south.

In the south, the Basin Ranges shimmer with heat even during winter. Here in the north, though, cattlemen use axes to chop holes in the snow-rippled ice of ponds. Cattle plod through rolling white fields, leaders breaking a muddy trail through the snow while calves struggle to keep up. Farmhouses and horses alike huddle beneath scattered trees. Mule deer lie in the foothills, waiting for dark to venture down into the bottomlands and snow-capped haystacks of the Pit River. Their huge ears rise above the sagebrush like black stumps.

Most Basin Ranges in northeastern California, except for the Warner Mountains, are not ranges at all, but prominent mountains and their shoulders and ridges. Bald-topped Observation

Mono Lake (left), as seen from Mt. Lewis, receives its waters from both the Sierra Nevada and the Basin Ranges. GEORGE WUERTHNER

Shooting stars with their small pink rockets of blossoms line Pine Creek Basin (opposite page) in the 69,000-acre South Warner Wilderness. Trails in the South Warner Wilderness are designed for access and penetration only—once hikers reach the wilderness area, they must bushwhack.
JEFF GNASS

Peak (7,964 feet) and McDonald Peak (7,931 feet) are the largest of these. Near Susanville, osprey feed beneath Fredonyer Peak (7,943 feet), where only one kind of fish, Eagle trout, inhabits alkaline Eagle Lake.

The Warners, however, are a quite impressive range, forming a sixty-mile long, twenty-mile wide rampart in the northeastern corner of the state. The eastern, steeper slopes of the range are barren, blanketed with sage and grasses, interspersed with lonely stands and canyon-bottom fingers of pine, juniper, and aspen. The long western slopes drain more moisture from Pacific storms, however, and nourish large forestlands, rolling grazing land, and the headwaters of the Pit River.

The Warners are crossed by only one paved road, at Cedar Pass. A single, small ski resort operates here, the only facility anywhere within the Warners, testimony to their isolation from California's population centers. Pickups wait at lonely highway intersections, miles from the nearest building, for the school bus.

Yet these mountains are rich with rugged scenery and impressive vantage points. A hiking trail along the Warner backbone gives access to the highest and most extensively glaciated summits in the range—Eagle Peak (9,892 feet), Warren Peak (9,710 feet), and Hat Mountain (8,737 feet)—four thousand feet above the plateaus beneath and within easy sight of Mt. Shasta and Lassen Peak in the Cascades. Patches of ponderosa, limber, and whitebark pines interrupt grassy meadows and basins in the 69,000-acre South Warner Wilderness surrounding Eagle Peak, and alpine lakes and splashing streams attract summertime anglers willing to bushwhack their way in. Sprawling Goose Lake below, often frozen silver, extends imperceptibly into Oregon.

Desert primrose (left) lends its elegant white petals and sand verbena contributes a rich, sweet fragrance to bring beauty out of sandy, inhospitable soils. LEO L. LARSON

Smooth, graceful sand dunes contrast with the rugged peaks of the Cottonwood Mountains (right) on the west side of Death Valley. Dunes consist of amazingly uniform grains of durable sand (about seven-thousandths of an inch in diameter), since smaller particles are whisked completely away from the desert by winds and larger particles are too difficult for the wind to move. TOM BEAN

A conclusion:

Beyond the horizon

According to legend and Bret Harte, Mount Diablo was named for the Devil following one of those crucial meetings between Good and Evil which always seem (like the stories of geologists) to explain the present.

According to the legend a Spanish priest, Father Jose Haro, was zealously expanding the frontiers of the Holy Church in California, causing some discomfort to Satan. In 1770, Father Jose began another missionary expedition, which took him to the summit of Mount Diablo and its spectacular view. "Each little knoll in fancy became crowned with a chapel; from each dark canyon gleamed the white walls of a mission building. . . . He already saw the spires of stately cathedrals, the domes of palaces, vineyards, gardens and groves."

The Arch-Fiend appeared, however, and interrupted Father Jose's romantic vision to tell him that his missionary zeal was wasted. Then Satan showed Father Jose a quite different vision of the future. To the west of Mount Diablo, gallant Spanish cavaliers and dedicated churchmen were streaming toward waiting ships, leaving California.

To the east of Mount Diablo, streaming through the passes of snowy mountains, appeared "a strange and motley crew. . . pushing, bustling, panting, and swaggering. And as they passed, the good Father noticed that giant trees were prostrated as with the breath of a tornado, and the bowels of the earth were torn and rent as with a convulsion." They carried no cross, but only the effigy of a bear—the symbol of the Devil.

Then Satan took Father Jose beneath the earth, where subterranean creatures were carrying ladles filled with liquid gold and bound for the surface.

"But listen, Sir Priest," the Devil bargained. "It lies with you to avert the issue for a time. Leave me here in peace. . .and you shall not lack that which will render your old age an ornament and a blessing."

Father Jose, of course, could not be bribed. "Diabolus, I defy thee!" he shouted. There was a fierce struggle, and when the Padre regained consciousness, he was being carried by disciples on a stretcher after having been mauled by a monstrous bear.

The Father recovered, continued his vigorous proselytizing, and the rest, for better or worse, is the history of California's mountains. Perhaps, had Father Jose been less resolute and more pragmatic, perhaps if he had bargained with the Devil, the

One of the most famous trees in California, this gnarled Jeffrey pine (left) on Sentinel Dome in Yosemite National Park attests vividly to the brutality of high-altitude winds. By a process known as "wind pruning" the windward leaves, sprigs, and branches of a tree are killed by dehydration and the blast of tiny ice and snow particles. New growth survives only where it is protected—even if the only shelter is provided by dead parts of the tree itself. LINDA WEEKS

Glorious sunset silhouettes the Minarets, a cluster of spectacular needles and shattered rock in the Ritter Range. MICHAEL S. SAMPLE

mountains of California would be more peaceful and less controversial today. Perhaps grizzly bears would not have vanished.

Yet, a chapel on every mountain is no more preferable to many Californians than hydraulic mining. For some reason, the Arch-Fiend seems to triumph even when we, like Father Jose, shout our defiance. Somehow, the future of California's mountains seems inevitable.

More importantly, the mountains of California determine *our* future, *our* horizons. Our concern for the mountains is concern for ourselves. California's mountains hold the keys to the state's future. They offer water, timber, and minerals. They confront us with pollution, erosion, and difficult transportation. They will not be ignored.

Anyone who spends time in California's mountains understands how many ways the earth can meet the sky. With each new step in the mountains, the horizon changes. Here, it looms directly overhead, jagged and foreboding. There, it fades into the distance—beautiful and enchanting.

In the same way, California alters its future with every new step into the mountains. Here, cutting, mining, and building seem to leave the mountains more ragged. There, the mountains seem to resist, destroying homes and highways, people and predictions. In a few more years...

For California's mountains, there is no such thing as "a few more years." It is *we* who are so short-lived. Horizons change in relation to us, not the mountains. We need California's mountains far more desperately than they need us. And they do not need our protection or help. We do.

In a very real sense, California's mountain ranges are above all that.

Yosemite's El Capitan, seen from Taft Point, catches the last sliver of evening light. PAT O'HARA

Nature can paint the most beautiful pictures, such as this reflection of the Sierra Nevada's Ragged Peak in Young Lake, one of the thousands of alpine lakes scattered throughout the mountains of California. CHARLIE BORLAND

MOUNTAIN TRIVIA

There is always, it seems, so much to tell about California's mountain ranges—too much, at least, to fit between the covers of a book. But who can resist trying?

This section includes those delicious, assorted morsels of information guaranteed to satisfy the appetite of the most starved devotee of California mountains. The alphabetical listing of every mountain range in California,

for instance, and the list of the state's one hundred highest peaks offer a bonanza of distilled and fascinating data that until now has not been collected in one book.

Some facts in this section don't seem to go with each other. For example, the only apparent relation between the first automobile to enter Yosemite Valley and the first fatality atop Mt. Whitney is the fact that both events were

the first of their kind. Either fact might have fit nicely in a previous chapter. But regrettably, interesting details, such as the following, became the leftovers when the main chapters of *California Mountain Ranges* were completed. Still, they seem too hard-earned, too valuable to throw away.

So here are the leftovers—some significant, some not, last but not least.

The mountain ranges of California, a summary

The following list of California mountain ranges was compiled using USGS maps and USGS computer lists. It includes only those mountain formations officially designated as ranges—not formations designated as ridges, hills, rocks, and the like.

AGUA TIBIA MOUNTAINS—Located in the Peninsular Ranges northwest of Mt. Palomar, these mountains are protected within the fifteen-square-mile Agua Tibia Wilderness. Eagle Crag (5,077 feet) is the tallest peak in the wilderness; USGS listings, however, consider Palomar Mountain (6,140 feet) the highest peak in the range.

AMARGOSA RANGE—This major Basin Range consists of several smaller ranges, including the Funeral and Black mountains. Pyramid Peak (6,703 feet) in the Funeral Mountains is the highest of the Amargosa peaks.

ARGUS RANGE—Located east of the Panamints, this Basin Range reaches its highest point at 8,839-foot Maturango Peak.

AVAWATZ MOUNTAINS—A Basin Range nearly thirty miles in length, the Avawatz Mountains are located northwest of Baker. Highest peak is 6,154 feet.

BENTON RANGE—Southeast of Mono Lake, the

Bentons look across the Owens River at eye-level with the Sierras. Glass Mountain, highest in the range, is 11,123 feet.

BIG MARIA MOUNTAINS—The Big Marias are a twenty-mile-long Basin Range located just north of Blythe, on the Arizona border. The USGS lists the maximum elevation as 3,375 feet; most maps, however, show the tallest peak to be 2,870 feet.

BIG VALLEY MOUNTAINS—Located in the northern segment of the Basin Ranges, the Big Valley Mountains are the westernmost Basin Range north of the Sierras. Highest elevation is 5,086 feet west of Fall River Mills and Macarthur.

BRISTOL MOUNTAINS—This thirty-five-mile-long Basin Range is seen by thousands of motorists north of U.S. 66 and Amboy. Highest elevations reach 3,609 feet.

BULLION MOUNTAINS—Nearly forty miles in length, this Basin Range is located north of Twenty-nine Palms in the Mojave Desert. Highest elevation is 4,187 feet.

CADY MOUNTAINS—A smaller Basin Range located west of the Bristol Mountains, the Cady Mountains reach 4,627 feet in elevation.

CALICO MOUNTAINS—A tiny cluster of Basin Range mountains rising above Barstow, the Calicos

never reach above 3,500 feet in elevation.

CALIENTE RANGE—These barren, rugged South Coast Range mountains stretch more than thirty miles between the Cuyama Valley and the Carrizo Plain. Caliente Mountain (5,106 feet) is highest in the range.

CARGO MUCHACHO MOUNTAINS—This tiny Basin Range, less than ten miles in circumference, rises from the desert in the extreme southeast corner of California. The Cargo Muchachos, located northwest of Winterhaven and Interstate 8, reach a maximum elevation of 2,225 feet.

CASCADE RANGE—Its two highest California peaks, Mt. Shasta (elev. 14,162 feet) and Lassen Peak (elev. 10,457 feet), dominate the landscape for miles beyond this volcanic range, which divides the Sierra Nevada from the Klamaths.

CASTLE MOUNTAINS—The Castles, a Basin Range immediately south of the New York Mountains on the Nevada border, reach a maximum elevation of 5,550 feet.

CATHEDRAL RANGE—Actually a sub-range of the Sierra Nevada, the Cathedral Range is a series of peaks west of the Sierra crest where the Tuolumne River begins. The Cathedral Range joins the main crest at Mt. Lyell (13,114 feet), which is usually considered its highest peak.

CHEMEHUEVI MOUNTAINS—Located south of the Sacramento Mountains, these peaks culminate in Chemehuevi Peak (elev. 3,697 feet) at their southern end.

CHOCOLATE MOUNTAINS—One of the larger Basin Ranges, this narrow string of peaks stretches for sixty miles directly east of Salton Sea. Highest elevation is 2,700 feet above sea level.

CHUCKWALLA MOUNTAINS—Located northeast of Salton Sea, just beyond the Chocolate Mountains, this Basin Range reaches an elevation of 4,504 feet at Black Butte.

CLARK MOUNTAIN RANGE—Clark Mountain (7,929 feet) dominates this Basin Range, north of Interstate 15 at the Nevada border.

CLIPPER MOUNTAINS—A minor ridge of peaks southeast of the Providence Mountains, the Clippers reach their highest point at 4,604 feet.

COSO RANGE—South of Owens Lake and across U.S. 395 from the Sierra Nevada, this Basin Range reaches its highest point at Coso Peak (8,160 feet).

COTTONWOOD MOUNTAINS—Located east of the Inyo Mountains, this forty-mile-long Basin Range is often considered part of the Panamint Range, although separated by Towne Pass from the major crest of that range. Tin Mountain (8,953 feet) is the highest in the Cottonwoods.

COXCOMB MOUNTAINS—North of Desert Center on Interstate 10, the Coxcombs are less than twenty miles long, never reaching higher than 4,450 feet.

COYOTE MOUNTAINS—North of Ocotillo, this Peninsular Range extends about ten miles east of

Cactus and oak dot the east end of Santa Catalina Island, which is actually a ridge of offshore peaks belonging to the Penisular Ranges. JEFF GNASS

the Jacumba Mountains and Sweeney Pass. Highest elevation is 2,408 feet.

DIABLO RANGE—Although not extremely high, the mountains of this range extend for nearly 175 miles from San Francisco Bay to the Temblor Range, and are nearly thirty miles wide in places. Highest peak in the range is San Benito Mountain at 5,241 feet, although USGS lists highest elevation in the range at 5,258 feet.

DIAMOND MOUNTAINS—Stretching fifty miles south of Honey Lake, the crest of these mountains in the northern portion of the Basin Ranges forms part of the boundary between Plumas and Lassen counties. Thompson Peak (7,795 feet) and Adams Peak (8,197 feet) are the highest points along this county line, but Dixie Mountain (8,323 feet) is highest in the range.

EAGLE MOUNTAINS—The Eagles meet the southeastern tip of the Little San Bernardino Mountains and thus mark the boundary of the Basin Ranges. Top elevation is 5,350 feet.

EL PASO MOUNTAINS—This Basin Range nearly intersects the southern Sierra south of Ridgecrest. Highest peak is 4,578 feet above sea level.

FUNERAL MOUNTAINS—Often considered part of the Amargosa Range, the Funerals parallel the Nevada border east of the town of Death Valley. Highest point in this Basin Range is Pyramid Peak at an elevation of 6,703 feet.

GABILAN RANGE—The Gabilans, facing the Sierra de Salinas for forty miles across the Salinas Valley, are one of the rugged South Coast Ranges. Mt. Johnson (3,454 feet) is the highest summit in the range.

GRANITE MOUNTAINS—There are actually four Basin Ranges by this name. One, a small ridge at the north end of the Palen Mountains, northeast of the Coxcomb Mountains, reaches a highest elevation of 4,353 feet. A second, east of Victorville, includes Sidewinder Mountain (5,272 feet) as its highest peak. A third, south of the Owlshead Mountains, reaches 5,299 feet elevation. And a fourth, southwest of the Providence Mountains (and across one of several Granite Passes) reaches an elevation of 6,738 feet.

GRAPEVINE MOUNTAINS—Often considered part of the Amargosa Range, these Basin Range mountains parallel the Nevada border just north of Death Valley, reaching 8,450 feet at their highest level.

GREENHORN MOUNTAINS—These southwestern Sierra Nevada peaks form the prominent ridge west of Isabella Reservoir. Tobias Peak (8,284 feet) is often considered the highest of the Greenhorn Mountains. However, their northern border is unclear, and the USGS lists highest elevation at 8,320 feet.

GREENWATER RANGE—The Greenwaters are east of Death Valley, tucked behind the Black Mountains. Maximum elevation is 5,148 feet.

GRIZZLY MOUNTAINS—Located in Plumas County in the northern Sierra Nevada, southeast of Lake Almanor, the USGS lists maximum elevation in the Grizzlies at 7,878 feet.

INYO MOUNTAINS—Almost as high as the White Mountains to the north, the rugged, barren Inyos face Mt. Whitney and the Sierra across Owens Valley. Waucoba Mountain (11,123 feet) is the highest summit in the range.

IRON MOUNTAINS—The Iron Mountains, a ten-mile-by-five-mile Basin Range located north of the Granite Mountains (the range by that name east of Joshua Tree National Monument) and Granite Pass, reach a top elevation of 3,350 feet.

IVANPAH MOUNTAINS—Rising immediately north of Cima, these Basin Range mountains reach their pinnacle at Kessler Peak (6,163 feet).

JACUMBA MOUNTAINS—Stretching north from the Mexican border between the Interstate 8 towns of Live Oak Springs and Ocotillo, the Jacumbas reach 4,647 feet at Mt. Tule.

KING RANGE—Often known as California's "Lost Coast" because its rugged mountains force the Coastal Highway (California 1) inland, these North Coast Range mountains reach 4,087 feet at King Mountain, plunging spectacularly to the ocean, a dramatic relief that rivals any in the Sierra Nevada.

KINGSTON RANGE—Kingston Peak (7,323 feet) is the highest in this range south of Death Valley near the Nevada border.

LAGUNA MOUNTAINS—A Peninsular Range located east of San Diego near the town of Mt. Laguna, with Monument Peak (6,271 feet) its highest.

LA PANZA RANGE—East of San Luis Obispo Mountains, the La Panzas extend forty miles north of the Sierra Madre and Caliente mountains. Branch Mountain (3,770 feet) is the highest peak with a name, but the USGS lists the top elevation of the La Panzas as 4,054 feet.

LAST CHANCE RANGE—A Basin Range stretching south for nearly forty miles from the Nevada border and just east of the White and Inyo mountains. Dry Mountain (8,674 feet) is the highest peak with an official name, but the USGS lists the highest elevation in the range at 8,726 feet.

LITTLE MARIA MOUNTAINS—Located just west of the Big Marias, with the town of Midland in between, these Basin Range mountains reach a top elevation of 3,035 feet.

LITTLE SAN BERNARDINO MOUNTAINS—The easternmost of the Transverse Ranges, the Little San Bernardinos are sometimes considered a Basin Range. Situated north of famous Salton Sea, they reach an elevation of 5,814 feet at Quail Mountain.

MARBLE MOUNTAINS—Famous among spelunkers for their extensive network of marble caves, most of these Klamath Range mountains are protected within the Marble Mountain Wilderness. The USGS lists the highest elevation of the range at 8,317 feet.

MARBLE MOUNTAINS—The Basin Range Marble Mountains rise south of the Providence Mountains and Interstate 40. Maximum elevation is 3,842 feet.

MAYACAMAS MOUNTAINS—One of the North Coast Ranges, these mountains extend for about fifty miles west of Clear Lake. Most famous for geothermal developments, The Geysers, near Cobb Mountain, the Mayacamas reach their highest point at Mt. St. Helena (4,343 feet).

NEW YORK MOUNTAINS—These are among the highest Basin Range peaks south of the Death Valley region. Highest elevation is 7,532 feet.

NOPAH RANGE—On the Nevada border southeast of Death Valley, the Nopahs trend south for more than thirty miles. The USGS lists highest point as 6,415 feet above sea level, but most maps indicate a peak of 6,394 feet is tops.

OAK RIDGE MOUNTAINS—This Transverse Ranges ridge curves for nearly forty miles north of the Santa Monica Mountains and northwest of Los Angeles. Oat Mountain (3,747 feet) at the eastern extreme of the ridge is the highest peak.

OLD WOMAN MOUNTAINS—Located in the Basin Ranges, the range lies southwest of Needles and reaches a maximum elevation of 5,090 feet.

OROCOPIA MOUNTAINS—This is the Basin Range overlooking the Salton Sea from the north, reaching an elevation of 3,815 feet.

OWLSHEAD MOUNTAINS—These interesting Basin Range mountains form nearly a full circle at the southern end of Death Valley. Maximum elevation is 4,408 feet.

PALEN MOUNTAINS—The Palens are a small Basin Range formation which join with the Granite Mountains to the north in forming a semi-circle northeast of Desert Center. Highest elevation is 3,851 feet.

PANAMINT RANGE—Among the largest Basin Ranges in terms of area, the Panamints tower above Death Valley to the east. Telescope Peak (11,049 feet), highest in the ninety-mile-long range, looks out on the lowest (Badwater, Death Valley) and highest (Mt. Whitney) elevations in the lower 48 states.

PINTO MOUNTAINS—East of the Little San Bernardinos, this Basin Range is generally considered

Fall color helps brighten the slopes of majestic Mt. Dana in the Sierra Nevada. MICHAEL S. SAMPLE

the dividing line between the Colorado Desert to the south and Mojave Desert to the north. Highest elevation is 4,650 feet, according to the USGS; other maps show Twentynine Palms Mountain (4,562 feet) to be the tallest in the range.

PIUTE RANGE—The Piutes, a Basin Range, rise to 4,909 feet north of Needles on the Nevada border. A ridge of the southern Sierra Nevada, located between the Greenhorn and Scodie Mountains, is also known as the Piute Mountains.

PORTAL RIDGE MOUNTAINS—The Portal Ridge overlooks the Antelope Valley between Palmdale and the Tehachapis. Burt Peak (5,788 feet) is often considered the highest mountain on the Portal Ridge, although it is actually located somewhat southwest.

PROVIDENCE MOUNTAINS—Best known for Mitchell Caverns, the deep limestone caves located on their eastern slopes, the Providence Mountains north of Amboy and U.S. 66 extend forty miles and reach their highest point at 7,171-foot Mt. Edgar.

QUAIL MOUNTAINS—This is a minor Basin Range cluster of mountains at the southern tip of the Panamint Range, reaching 5,103 feet above sea level.

RAND MOUNTAINS—The Rands are a tiny Basin Range rising south of Randsburg and the El Paso Mountains. Highest elevation is 4,740 feet.

RITTER RANGE—Like the Cathedral Range directly north, the Ritters are a sub-range of the Sierra Nevada. The two great sentinels of the range, Mt. Ritter (13,157 feet) and Banner Peak (12,945 feet) are especially prominent because the Sierra Nevada crest to the east is actually thousands of feet lower.

RIVERSIDE MOUNTAINS—Actually a two-part Basin Range, the compact Riversides near the Arizona border south of Vidal Junction consist of the Riverside Mountains (2,252 feet maximum) and the West Riverside Mountains (2,667 feet maximum).

SACRAMENTO MOUNTAINS—Eagle Peak (3,308 feet) is the highest of the Sacramentos, which rise above U.S. 66 west of Needles.

SALMON MOUNTAINS—Among the most isolated mountains in California, these peaks occupy the heart of the Klamath Ranges region and are centered around Sawyers Bar. Bordered on the southeast by the Trinity Alps and on the north by the Marble and Scott Bar mountains, the Salmons reach an elevation of 8,196 feet at Russian Peak.

SAN BERNARDINO MOUNTAINS—The major and most popular Transverse Range, the San Bernardinos extend more than fifty miles from Interstate 15 and Cajon Junction to San Gorgonio Pass and Palm Wells. Big Bear Lake and its complex of resorts are here, in the shadow of massive San Gorgonio Mountain (11,502 feet), the highest peak in the Transverse Ranges and all of Southern California.

SAN GABRIEL MOUNTAINS—Towering Mt. San Antonio (10,064 feet) above the Los Angeles Basin is the tallest peak in this Transverse Range. Extending from San Fernando Pass in the west to Interstate 15 in the east, the San Gabriels are twenty-five miles wide at their broadest and witness terrible mudslides and terrific snow skiing almost every year.

SAN JACINTO MOUNTAINS—Topped by the highest peak in the Peninsular Ranges—San Jacinto Peak (10,804 feet) above Palm Springs—these desolate mountains are bounded by San Gorgonio Pass in the north and the Santa Rosa Mountains in the south.

SAN RAFAEL MOUNTAINS—Between the Sierra Madres of the South Coast Ranges and the Santa Ynez Mountains of the Transverse Ranges, the San Rafaels form a transition between the two mountain regions. They are generally regarded as a South Coast Range, however, with Big Pine Mountain rising to 6,828 feet. The USGS lists maximum elevation at 6,880 feet.

SAN YSIDRO MOUNTAINS—Located in the Peninsular Ranges, these mountains on the Mexican border near San Diego reach a top elevation of 3,572 feet.

SANTA ANA MOUNTAINS—One of the Peninsular Ranges, the Santa Anas southeast of Los Angeles have lent their name to the hot desert winds that funnel past them during summer, baking millions of urban Californians. Santiago Peak (5,687 feet) is the highest in the Santa Anas.

SANTA CRUZ MOUNTAINS—From San Francisco, the Santa Cruz Mountains widen to Santa Cruz and Gilroy, bounded by the Pacific Ocean on the west and the Santa Clara Valley on the east. At 3,791 feet, Loma Prieta is by far the highest peak of this chain in the South Coast Ranges.

SANTA LUCIA RANGE—For a hundred miles south of Monterey, the Santa Lucias create some of the most rugged and scenic terrain in all of California, including the Big Sur coastline. Junipero Serra Peak (5,862 feet) is the highest point in this South Coast Range.

SANTA MARGARITA MOUNTAINS—Located in Orange County, the USGS lists a maximum elevation of 3,189 feet for these Peninsular Range mountains.

SANTA MONICA MOUNTAINS—These mountains west of Los Angeles, part of the Transverse Ranges, were the site for filming of the television series M*A*S*H. Highest elevation is 2,836 feet.

SANTA ROSA MOUNTAINS—Northwest of Salton Sea, the Santa Rosa Mountains reach 8,716 feet at Toro Peak in the northern end of this Peninsular Range.

SANTA SUSANA MOUNTAINS—Located in Los Angeles County (although often omitted from maps), the Santa Susanas reach 3,756 feet at their highest.

SANTA YNEZ MOUNTAINS—This Transverse Ranges chain extends sixty miles along the coast from Point Concepcion, past Santa Barbara, to Ventura, Lake Casitas, and Ojai. The USGS lists the top elevation as 4,864 feet.

SCODIE MOUNTAINS—Actually part of the Sierra Nevada, the Scodie Mountains are located near the southern tip of the range, west of the town of Ridgecrest. The sub-range reaches its highest elevation of 7,046 feet above Walker Pass.

SCOTT BAR MOUNTAINS—Closing the Scott Valley in the north, the Scott Bar Mountains also overlook the upper Klamath River and Yreka. Gunsight Peak (6,146 feet) is the most visible in the Scott Bars; the USGS, however, lists highest elevation at 6,265 feet.

SCOTT MOUNTAINS—These Klamath Range mountains north of Clair Engle Lake form the southern wall of the pastoral Scott Valley. China Mountain (8,542 feet) southwest of Weed is the highest of the Scotts.

SHEEP HOLE MOUNTAINS—This small but rugged Basin Range is located east of Twentynine Palms. Maximum elevation is 4,613 feet.

SIERRA DE SALINAS—From Monterey and Salinas in the north, these South Coast Range mountains present a barren face above the Salinas Valley all the way to Soledad and Greenfield in the south. Their lower western slopes, however, help form the beautiful Carmel Valley. Palo Escrito Peak (4,467 feet), located midway in the range, is the highest elevation.

SIERRA MADRE MOUNTAINS—South of the dry Cuyama Valley and east of Santa Maria, the forty-mile-long Sierra Madres are the most southern of the major South Coast Ranges. Cuyama Peak (5,875 feet) is generally considered the highest elevation in the Sierra Madres.

SIERRA PELONA—Overlooking the Antelope Valley, this Transverse Ranges formation rises quickly to the west of Palmdale. Highest elevation is 5,187 feet.

SISKIYOU MOUNTAINS—These are the most northwestern mountains in California, and extend into Oregon. They are widely considered a sort of island in the Klamath Ranges due to the variety of plant and animal life found here and nowhere else. Preston Peak (7,310 feet) towers above every other peak around it and is the highest California peak in the Siskiyous.

SKEDADDLE MOUNTAINS—Overlooking Honey Lake from the east, this small cluster of

A camper beneath Banner Peak in the 107,000-acre Ansel Adams Wilderness (formerly the Minarets Wilderness) has one of the most stunning views in the Ritter Range.
CHARLIE BORLAND

mountains in the upper Basin Ranges is dominated by Hot Springs Peak (7,680 feet).

SLATE RANGE—This narrow string of Basin Ranges peaks extends more than twenty miles at the southern end of the Panamint Valley. Highest point is Straw Peak (5,578 feet).

SODA MOUNTAINS—Located just north of Interstate 15 at Baker, the highest peak in the Soda Mountains reaches an elevation of 3,617 feet and overlooks the empty, sandy bed of Soda Lake.

SOUTH FORK MOUNTAINS—Also called the South Fork Ridge, this prominent string of peaks separates the Klamath Range to the northeast from the North Coast Ranges to the southwest. Highest elevation is at Horse Ridge Lookout (6,070 feet).

SUTTER BUTTES—Perhaps the smallest distinct mountain range in the world, the Sutter Buttes fit conveniently in no other grouping of ranges. Rising near Marysville in the flat Sacramento Valley, they reach a top elevation of 2,132 feet.

SWEETWATER MOUNTAINS—These are the most northern Basin Range mountains in the southern portion of that divided region. Located north of Bridgeport, the Sweetwaters count Mt. Patterson (11,673 feet) as their highest peak.

TEHACHAPI MOUNTAINS—Although not part of the Transverse Ranges, it is often grouped with those ranges because of its atypical alignment. The Tehachapis join the Sierra Nevada (geologically more closely related) to the Transverse Ranges. Double Mountain (7,981 feet) is the tallest peak.

TEMBLOR RANGE—This thin string of peaks west of Bakersfield forms the foreboding barrier of the San Joaquin Valley for approximately eighty miles. McKittrick Summit (4,332 feet) is the highest point in the range.

TIEFORT MOUNTAINS—Tiny in extent, the Tiefort Mountains are less than ten miles in length and consist of one major peak 5,043 feet high, located east of Fort Irwin.

TOPATOPA MOUNTAINS—Located in the jumble of mountains where the South Coast Ranges meet the Tehachapis and Transverse Ranges, the Topatopas are often considered to include the Pine Mountain area which reaches an elevation of 7,510 feet at Reyes Peak north of Sespe Creek Canyon.

TRINITY ALPS—Frequently distinguished from the Trinity Mountains, "the Alps" nevertheless occupy the same region of the Klamath Ranges. Clustered closely together, the four major peaks resemble the grandest Sierra peaks. Highest of the Trinity Alps are Thompson Peak at 9,002 feet and Mt. Hilton at 8,964 feet.

TRINITY MOUNTAINS—East of the Trinity Divide. Highest point in this range is Mt. Eddy (9,025 feet).

TURTLE MOUNTAINS—This relatively short, twenty-mile-long Basin Range chain of mountains is located northeast of Vidal. Highest elevation is 4,313 feet.

VALLECITO MOUNTAINS—Southwest of the famous Salton Sea, the Vallecitos are twenty miles north of Agua Caliente Springs. Highest point is 5,348 feet.

WARNER RANGE—A major formation in the northern Basin Range also correctly classified as belonging to the volcanic Modoc Plateau, in extreme northeastern California. The fault-block Warners reach their highest point at 9,892-foot Eagle Peak.

WHIPPLE MOUNTAINS—Rising 4,131 feet above sea level, these mountains are the easternmost mountains in California, located near Parker Dam and Lake Havasu on the Arizona border.

WHITE MOUNTAINS—These towering Basin Range peaks stretch north for forty miles from the Owens Valley, challenging the High Sierra in elevation. Although scenic and diverse throughout,

the White Mountains are probably best known for the 4,600-year-old bristlecone pine growing there. The White Mountains are also quite high, reaching an elevation of 14,246 feet above sea level at White Mountain Peak.

YOLLA BOLLY MOUNTAINS—Serving as a buffer between the Klamath and North Coast ranges—and bearing similarities to each area—the Yolla Bollys are often divided into the North Yolla Bollys topped by North Yolla Bolly Peak (7,863 feet), belonging to the Klamath Ranges, and the South Yolla Bollys containing South Yolla Bolly Peak (8,092 feet), belonging to the North Coast Ranges.

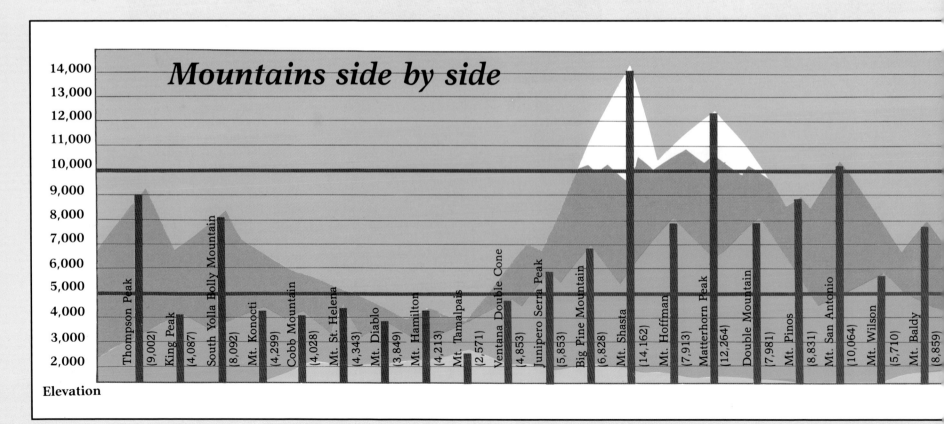

Mountains side by side

Elevation

14,000
13,000
12,000
11,000
10,000
9,000
8,000
7,000
6,000
5,000
4,000
3,000
2,000

Thompson Peak (9,002) · King Peak (4,087) · South Yolla Bolly Mountain (8,092) · Mt. Konocti (4,299) · Cobb Mountain (4,028) · Mt. St. Helena (4,343) · Mt. Diablo (3,849) · Mt. Hamilton (4,213) · Mt. Tamalpais (2,571) · Ventana Double Cone (4,853) · Junipero Serra Peak (5,853) · Big Pine Mountain (6,828) · Mt. Shasta (14,162) · Mt. Hoffman (7,913) · Matterhorn Peak (12,264) · Double Mountain (7,981) · Mt. Pinos (8,831) · Mt. San Antonio (10,064) · Mt. Wilson (5,710) · Mt. Baldy (8,859)

Mountain firsts

FIRST DESCRIPTION OF SIERRA NEVADA—Padre Fray Juan Crespi, in diary entry as he accompanied Captain Pedro Fages expedition in 1772.

FIRST OVERLAND CROSSING OF HIGH SIERRA—Jedediah Smith, Silas Gobel, and Robert Evans, at Ebbetts Pass, May 1827 (traveling west to east).

FIRST EAST-WEST CROSSING OF SIERRA—Joseph Reddeford Walker expedition in 1833.

FIRST AMERICAN SETTLERS TO CROSS THE SIERRA NEVADA—John Bartelson-John Bidwell party in 1834. This expedition included first woman, Nancy Kelsey, and first child, Ann Kelsey, to cross Sierra Nevada.

FIRST RECORDED ASCENT OF MAJOR SIERRA PEAK—William Brewer, Charles Hoffman, and Josiah Whitney, Mt. Hoffman, 1863.

FIRST MENTION OF GIANT SEQUOIA—Zenas Leonard, member of Joseph Reddeford Walker expedition, in Pennsylvania newspaper in 1835 (two years after expedition encountered trees).

FIRST ASCENT OF MT. WHITNEY—A.H. Johnson, C.P. Begole, and John Lucas, Aug. 18, 1873.

FIRST PHOTOGRAPHER TO SCALE MT. WHITNEY—W.E. James of New York, 1873

FIRST WOMEN TO SCALE MT. WHITNEY—Anna Mills, Hope Broughton, Mary Martin, and M. Redd, 1878.

FIRST FATALITY ON MT. WHITNEY—Byrd Surby, killed by lightning after attaining summit, July 26, 1904.

FIRST ESTABLISHED SKI RESORT IN CALIFORNIA—Badger Pass above Yosemite Valley, opened in 1935.

FIRST WHITE MEN TO SEE YOSEMITE—Joseph Reddeford Walker expedition in 1833.

FIRST PARTY OF YOSEMITE TOURISTS—1855.

FIRST ASCENT OF YOSEMITE'S HALF DOME—George C. Anderson, 1875.

FIRST AUTOMOBILE IN YOSEMITE—Stanley Steamer, driven by A.E. Holmes and F.H. Holmes, July 1900.

FIRST RECORDED MENTION OF LAKE TAHOE—Lt. John C. Fremont, U.S. Topographical Engineers, on Feb. 14, 1843, after "an extraordinary dinner—pea soup, mule, and dog" the previous night.

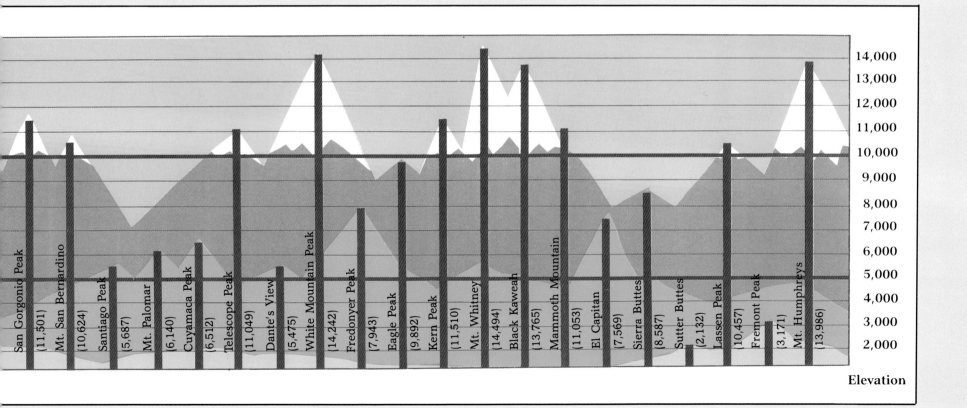

Elevation

Above all else: the 100 highest peaks in California

The following list of California's peak elevations, the official names of those peaks, the ranges in which they are located, and the first recorded ascents is based upon computerized lists provided by the United States Geographic Survey, on Sierra Club archives (including *The Climber's Guide to the High Sierra*, by Steve Roper, Sierra Club Books, 1976), and on the archives of the American Alpine Club.

Omitted from this list are peaks without official names, and peaks for which no exact elevation is available (such as Aperture Peak in the Sierra Nevada, listed on topographic maps as having an elevation of 13,200+).

It is also worth noting that many elevation figures were first recorded years ago and may not be exact. Moreover, California's mountain peaks are actually changing their elevations frequently—the 1872 Lone Pine (Owens Valley) earthquake, for example, raised numerous mountains in the Sierra Nevada several feet, and the 1971 San Fernando earthquake raised peaks in the Transverse Ranges a similar amount.

Elevation	Name	Location	First Ascent · Date
14,494	Mt. Whitney	Sierra Nevada	A.H. Johnson, C.P. Begole, and John Lucas, 1873
14,375	Mt. Williamson	Sierra Nevada	W.L. Hunter and C. Mulholland, 1884
14,246	White Mountain Peak	White Mts.	first ascent unknown
14,242	North Palisade	Sierra Nevada	James Hutchinson, Joseph N. Le Conte, and J.K. Moffitt, 1903
14,163	Mt. Sill	Sierra Nevada	James Hutchinson, Joseph N. Le Conte, James Moffitt, and Robert Pike, 1903
14,162	Mt. Shasta	Cascades	E.D. Pearce, 1854
14,086	Mt. Russell	Sierra Nevada	Norman Clyde, 1926
14,058	Split Mountain	Sierra Nevada	Frank Saulque and others, 1887
14,040	Middle Palisade	Sierra Nevada	Francis Farquhar and Ansel Hall, 1921
14,027	Mt. Langley	Sierra Nevada	first ascent unknown, but prior to 1871
14,018	Mt. Tyndall	Sierra Nevada	Clarence King and Richard Cotter, 1864
14,015	Mt. Muir	Sierra Nevada	John Mendenhall, Nelson Nies, 1935
14,000	Thunderbolt Peak	Sierra Nevada	Robert L.M. Underhill, Jules Eichorn, Lewis Clark, Norman Clyde, Glen Dawson, Francis Farquhar, and Bestor Robinson, 1931
13,990	Mt. Barnard	Sierra Nevada	John Hunter, William Hunter, and C. Mulholland, 1892
13,986	Mt. Humphreys	Sierra Nevada	G.R. Bunn and others, 1919
13,977	Mt. Keith	Sierra Nevada	C.G. Bradley, R.M. Price, J.C. Shinn, and J.E. Price, 1898
13,963	Mt. Stanford	Sierra Nevada	Bolton Boit Brown, 1896
13,960	Mt. Le Conte	Sierra Nevada	Norman Clyde, 1925
13,950	Trojan Peak	Sierra Nevada	Norman Clyde, 1926
13,917	Disappointment Peak	Sierra Nevada	J.M. Davies, A.L. Jordan, and H.H. Bliss, 1919
13,891	Mt. Agassiz	Sierra Nevada	Norman Clyde, 1925
13,888	Junction Peak	Sierra Nevada	E.B. Copeland and E.N. Henderson, 1899
13,850	Mt. Mallory	Sierra Nevada	Norman Clyde, 1925
13,832	Caltech Peak	Sierra Nevada	Norman Clyde, 1926
13,830	Mt. Darwin	Sierra Nevada	E.C. Andrews and Willard Johnson, 1908
13,802	Mt. Kaweah	Sierra Nevada	William Wallace, James Wright, and F.H. Wates, 1881
13,770	Mt. Irvine	Sierra Nevada	Norman Clyde, 1925
13,768	Mt. Winchell	Sierra Nevada	H.C. Mansfield, J.N. Newell, and W.B. Putnam, 1923
13,765	Black Kaweah	Sierra Nevada	James Hutchinson, Onis Imis Brown, and Duncan McDuffie, 1920
13,760	Mt. Corcoran	Sierra Nevada	Howard Gates, 1933
13,748	Mt. Morgan	Sierra Nevada	Wheeler Survey Party, (probably), 1870
13,715	Mt. Abbot	Sierra Nevada	M. Yeatman and M.L. Huggins, 1927
13,713	Bear Creek Spire	Sierra Nevada	H.F. Ulrich, 1923
13,711	Mt. Gabb	Sierra Nevada	H.H. Bliss and A.L. Jordan, 1917
13,691	Mt. Mendel	Sierra Nevada	first ascent unknown, but prior to 1930
13,666	Midway Mountain	Sierra Nevada	Francis Farquhar, William Colby, Robert Price, and others, 1912
13,665	Birch Mountain	Sierra Nevada	J.W. Bledsoe, 1887
13,652	Mt. Tom	Sierra Nevada	Tom Clark (possibly), 1860

Elevation	Name	Location	First Ascent - Date
13,641	Milestone Mts.	Sierra Nevada	Francis Farquhar, William Colby, and Robert Price, 1912
13,632	University Peak	Sierra Nevada	Joseph N. Le Conte, Helen Gompertz, Estelle Miller, and Belle Miller, 1896
13,630	Table Mountain	Sierra Nevada	Paul Shoup, Fred Shoup, and Gilbert Hassel, 1908
13,608	Mt. Ericsson	Sierra Nevada	Bolton Coit Brown and Lucy Brown, 1896
13,588	Thunder Mountain	Sierra Nevada	George Davis, 1905
13,570	Mt. Brewer	Sierra Nevada	William Brewer and Charles Hoffman, 1864
13,568	Mt. Goddard	Sierra Nevada	Lil Winchell and Louis Davis, 1879
13,565	Tunnabora Peak	Sierra Nevada	George Davis, 1905
13,559	Mt. Dubois	White Mts.	first ascent unknown
13,552	Mt. Carillon	Sierra Nevada	Norman Clyde, 1925
13,538	Mt. Bolton Brown	Sierra Nevada	Chester Versteeg and Rudolph Berls, 1922
13,524	Mt. Fiske	Sierra Nevada	Charles N. Fiske, John Fiske, Stephen Fiske, and Frederick Kellet, 1922
13,510	Mt. Gayley	Sierra Nevada	Norman Clyde, 1927
13,495	Mt. Pinchot	Sierra Nevada	USGS members, 1905
13,485	Mt. Pickering	Sierra Nevada	Chester Versteeg, Tyler Van Degrift, and Oliver Kehrlein, 1936
13,484	The Jumpoff	White Mts.	first ascent unknown
13,470	Mt. Versteeg	Sierra Nevada	first ascent unknown
13,468	Mt. Mills	Sierra Nevada	James Hutchinson, Joseph N. Le Conte, and Duncan McDuffie, 1908
13,441	Montgomery Peak	White Mountains	first ascent unknown
13,435	Mt. Haeckel	Sierra Nevada	Rt. 1: Walter Huber and others, July 14, 1920; Rt. 5: Edward Allen, Francis Crofts, and Olcutt Haskell, July 14, 1920
13,417	Mt. Lamarck	Sierra Nevada	Norman Clyde, 1925
13,410	Mt. Newcomb	Sierra Nevada	Max Eckenburg and Bob Rumohr, 1936
13,397	Cardinal Mountain	Sierra Nevada	George Downing Jr., 1922
13,390	Mt. Jepson	Sierra Nevada	Don McGeein, Chet Errett, and Evelyn Errett, 1939
13,388	The Thumb	Sierra Nevada	W.B. Putnam, 1921
13,377	Mt. Wallace	Sierra Nevada	Theodore Solomons and E. Bonner, 1895
13,361	Mt. Hilgard	Sierra Nevada	Charles Urquhart, 1905
13,344	Mt. Jordan	Sierra Nevada	Art Argiewicz and others (probably), 1940; (Norman Clyde, lower summit probably, 1925)
13,330	Black Giant	Sierra Nevada	George Davis, 1905
13,329	Mt. Prater	Sierra Nevada	Fred Jones, 1948
13,327	North Guard	Sierra Nevada	Norman Clyde, 1925
13,325	Joe Devel Peak	Sierra Nevada	Wheeler Survey Party, 1875
13,289	Mt. Bradley	Sierra Nevada	J.E. Price, R.M. Price, J.C. Shinn, and C.B. Bradley, 1898
13,289	Black Mountain	Sierra Nevada	George Davis, 1905
13,271	Mt. McDuffie	Sierra Nevada	Charles Bays Locker, Karl Hufbauer, and Alfred Elkin, 1951
13,265	Deerhorn Mountain	Sierra Nevada	Norman Clyde (probably), 1927
13,253	Royce Peak	Sierra Nevada	Nathan Clark and Roy Crites, 1931
13,241	Gendarme Peak	Sierra Nevada	Andy Smatko and Bill Schuler, 1967
13,240	Basin Mountain	Sierra Nevada	Norman Clyde, 1937
13,231	Mt. Warlow (recently named)	Sierra Nevada	Nathaniel Goodrich and Marjory Hurd, 1926
13,225	Mt. Emerson	Sierra Nevada	Norman Clyde, 1926
13,224	South Guard	Sierra Nevada	Clarence King and Richard Cotter (probably), 1864
13,196	Mt. Julius Caesar	Sierra Nevada	A.H. Prater and Myrtle Prater, 1928
13,184	Mt. Hitchcock	Sierra Nevada	Frederick Wales, 1881
13,183	Acrodectes Peak	Sierra Nevada	Norman Clyde and others, 1935
13,183	Red Spur	Sierra Nevada	Jules Eichorn, Virginia Adams, Jane Younger, and Carl Jensen, 1936
13,179	Mt. Wynne	Sierra Nevada	Sierra Club group, 1935
13,177	Mt. Young	Sierra Nevada	Frederick Wales, William Wallace, and James Wright, 1881
13,169	Mt. Chamberlain	Sierra Nevada	J.H. Czock, date unknown
13,163	Red Slate Mountain	Sierra Nevada	James Gardiner (possibly), 1864
13,157	Mt. Ritter	Sierra Nevada	John Muir, 1872
13,126	Diamond Peak	Sierra Nevada	first ascent unknown
13,125	Mt. Baxter	Sierra Nevada	George Davis (probably), 1905
13,117	Mt. Huxley	Sierra Nevada	Norman Clyde, 1920
13,114	Mt. Lyell	Sierra Nevada	John Tileston, 1871
13,103	Mt. Gilbert	Sierra Nevada	Norman Clyde, 1928
13,092	Mt. Goode	Sierra Nevada	first ascent unknown
13,091	Charybdis	Sierra Nevada	Anna Dempster and John Dempster, 1931
13,077	Merriam Peak	Sierra Nevada	Lewis Clark, Julie Mortimer, and Ted Waller, 1933
13,075	Seven Gables	Sierra Nevada	Theodore Solomons and Leigh Bierce, 1894
13,055	Mt. Genevra	Sierra Nevada	Norman Clyde, 1925
13,053	Mt. Dana	Sierra Nevada	William Brewer and Charles Hoffman, 1863

CHARLES COZZENS

I live not in myself, but I become
portion of that around me; and to me
high mountains are a feeling, but the hum
of human cities torture.

—Lord Byron